The David & Charles Manual of
STOVES, HEARTHS AND CHIMNEYS

Keith Williams

The David & Charles Manual of
STOVES, HEARTHS AND CHIMNEYS

Keith Williams

David & Charles

A CIP record for this book is available from the British Library.

ISBN 0 7153 0019 0

First published 1987 (ISBN 0 7153 8795 2)
New edition 1992 (ISBN 0 7153 0019 0)

Typeset by XL Publishing Services, Nairn, Scotland
and printed in Great Britain by Redwood Press
Melksham   Wiltshire
for David & Charles
Brunel House, Newton Abbot, Devon

Contents

Introduction

This book describes the working of a machine that generates heat by burning the traditional fuels of coal, wood and peat, as well as the more modern fuels, oil and gas. This machine generates heat in a variety of ways, but its working principles are very simple and unchanging. The machine is the house. It creates heat by pulling in air from the exterior, using this oxygen supply to burn fuel and exhausting the resulting heat to the exterior. Some of the hot air escapes up the chimney and is vital in making the whole machine work. The remainder soaks through the fabric of the house. By utilising this 'soak-away' heat, comfortable temperatures within the living space are sustained. No part of this operation can be separated from the whole. The house functions as an entire heat-making engine.

Electricity is an exception to this heat system. Because it does not burn, and thereby consume oxygen and rely upon the intake of fresh air for its working modes, electricity is not strictly a fuel. This places electric heaters in a category of their own. Uniquely, such air ducting as they require is for the sole purpose of preserving the comfort and health of the householder.

With all other types of heater, the placing of the air intakes, the burning unit or stove and its associated distribution and heat storage unites, and the exhaust route to the exterior, are all of vital importance if the best use of the fuel's heat is to be realised.

Author's note: How to use this book

Find your particular problem or subject interest in the index. This will show you where to start reading. Thereafter, cross-references in the text will direct you to related subject matter in the book.

1 House Heating

Definition of Household Heat

A comfortable household heat is something we all understand, yet is difficult to define. It is somewhere between the extremes of heat and cold, although where that happy medium lies varies from individual to individual and from one tradition to another.

The Romans luxuriated in hot air fed through underfloor ducts. The Egyptains preferred the cold, believing that it brought the soul closer to heaven. The Knights of St George attributed to cold all the masculine virtues – vigour, strength, stamina and courage. Chinese emperors maintained cool palaces but covered themselves with layers of fur. George III attempted to strengthen his constitution by removing from Buckingham Palace almost all carpeting and 'other means of great warmth'. Queen Victoria, too, hated heat.

Le Corbusier, one of the founders of modern architecture, conceived houses that sustained a uniform climate all year round, and it is on this foundation that the present preoccupation with central heating rests. In effect, what we are setting out to achieve is the preservation of summer temperatures within the house as a stable and unchanging living environment.

As the proper working of the house as a heat-producing and a heat-using engine depends on the movement of air through its space, it is of vital importance to ensure that these are rigidly controlled to the point where heat extraction from fuel is at the highest efficiency and that heat loss from the chimney is kept to a minimum. This requirement is nowhere more strongly argued than in the consideration of open and closed fires and their relative performances.

Thermal comfort involves a balance in the house of warm air and radiant heat. Until 1980 it was not possible to define precisely thermal comfort. In that year, an American scientist, Dr P. O. Fanger, produced an equation that did so. This was later simplified and modified by Dr D. A. McIntyre as the result of studies made at The Coal Research Establishment. These can be expressed as a graph in which the heat/comfort factor is stated as: $(0.56t_A + 0.44t_R)$, °C, and the human metabolic raté (ie the rate at which the human body generates heat) as; QM, W/m^2. Tests were carried out on nude bodies, on those clad in underwear with lightweight trousers and shirt or skirt and blouse, and on those wearing underwear, business suit or skirt and thick sweater. These people were tested while seated, standing, walking and working at house cleaning.

The conclusions drawn from these complex statistics are most revealing.

1 'Comfort' areas in the house can be extended by improving house insulation (principally with cavity walls, double-glazing and loft-lining, although external shelter belts may also have a part to play (see p 26)). The comfort level is sustained even when the heat supply to the room is reduced to match the lower heat losses arising from the improved insulation.

2 The best level of thermal comfort in the room is achieved from radiant sources (ie a burning fire) rather than from appliances delivering convected warm air (ie a hot-water radiator). This is a surprising justification of traditional methods.

Early History of Fires

In man's earliest hut-like dwellings, the fire was placed on bare earth at the centre of the single room that served for both living and sleeping. As no provision was made for the smoke to escape, it found its way out through gaps in the poorly constructed walls and roof.

Later, when an entire community would be housed in the baronial hall, the communal fire was mounted on a plain brick or stone plinth. Slots were left in the roof for the smoke to escape through.

When the keep acquired a first-floor level, a new place had to be found for the fire which

Fig 1 Prince Rupert's fireplace, 1678

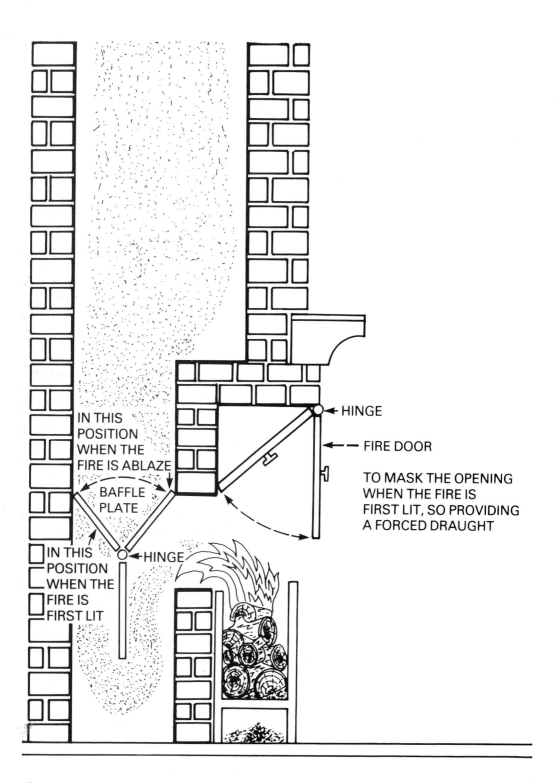

IN THIS
POSITION
WHEN THE
FIRE IS ABLAZE

BAFFLE
PLATE

IN THIS
POSITION
WHEN THE
FIRE IS
FIRST LIT

HINGE

HINGE

FIRE DOOR

TO MASK THE OPENING
WHEN THE FIRE IS
FIRST LIT, SO PROVIDING
A FORCED DRAUGHT

could not be lit on the wooden flooring. The fire's position was therefore transferred to a safe place in the stone wall where it was enclosed in an incombustible hearth. The escape flue ran horizontally through the wall. Gradually it was found that the fire burned more strongly, and less smoke escaped back into the hall, if the flue ran vertically.

Further generations passed before it was discovered that when the flue was raised above the roof in the form of a chimney the burning rate improved even further and smoke was prevented from being blown back into the living space by the wind's back pressure. Fires were used in this way up until the latter end of the seventeenth century.

Then, in 1678, Prince Rupert, nephew of Charles I, designed a fireplace that extracted additional heat from the fire gas before it escaped to the exterior. He placed his fire on a plinth in a metal basket, in front of a low wall in which was an opening (see illustration). Air could now flow into the fire from all sides and from beneath.

Behind the wall was a flue chamber divided by a cast-iron baffle plate mounted vertically. The top of the plate was hinged so that a section could be moved forwards and backwards, sealing off either the front or rear of the flue. When the fire was first lit, to obtain a maximum draught, the hinged section was pushed back to seal the rear half of the flue. Hot fire-gas rose straight up the chimney from the flue chamber.

As soon as the fire was at full heat, the baffle plate was pulled forward, sealing the front half of the chamber. Now the fire-gas was forced down to the base of the plate before curling round it to rise up as before. By restricting the air flow in this way, the fire's rate of burning could be regulated to some degree and more heat directed forwards into the living-room.

However, a brief consideration reveals the limitations of this design. Choking the fire-gas flow could cause a back pressure, forcing hot gas and smoke out into the living space. To prevent this and to improve the draught when lighting the fire, Prince Rupert fitted a hinged fire-door above the fire basket. This was hooked back during normal burning, but when the fire was being lit, or when smoke was escaping into the room, the door was locked down to act as a secondary baffle.

No further advances in fire control appeared for about a hundred years until towards the end of the eighteenth century, when Count Rumford of America created one of the two foundations on which modern fire design rests.

Prince Rupert's fireplace, with its hinged baffle, was inflexible because it had only two modes, a direct fire-gas flow up the chimney or an indirect flow around the baffle. Count Rumford argued that a variable control with 90° of movement would be superior. He therefore constructed a fireplace with a deep back wall of brick with its face sloping forward (see illustration). In the chimney throat – as wide as the chimney but no more than 75–100mm (3–4in) deep – he placed a metal closing plate, rotatable through a right angle so that the chimney could be closed, fully opened, or set for any position between. This arrangement also restrained down-draughts from the chimney terminal from forcing smoke by back pressure out into the living-room.

In addition, the chimney to which this fireplace was connected remained entirely within the house walls rather than running up the outside wall as had been the custom.

By these means Count Rumford improved control of the burning rate, pushed radiant heat forward into the living space (by sloping the back wall forward) and directed some of the fire's energy into the brick structure of the chimney, using it as a heat store.

Modern convector fires are based on Rumford's concepts.

Benjamin Franklin – American patriot, diplomat and amateur scientist – contributed greatly towards solving the remaining problems of stove control by creating the Pennsylvania fireplace (see illustration on p13).

The design was very simple. The fire burnt in the front of an enclosed chamber which was divided vertically (in much the same manner as Prince Rupert's fireplace) by a hollow baffle. This baffle was sealed from the fire chamber and connected only to the underfloor space beneath the stove. The fire also took its air from beneath the floor.

When the fire was lit, direct radiant heat was directed into the living-room. Fresh air was fed into it from the underfloor space, thus eliminating the draughts that for centuries had chilled the backs of those warming themselves in front of the fire.

As air within the sealed baffle was

Fig 2 Rumford Fireplace, late eighteenth century

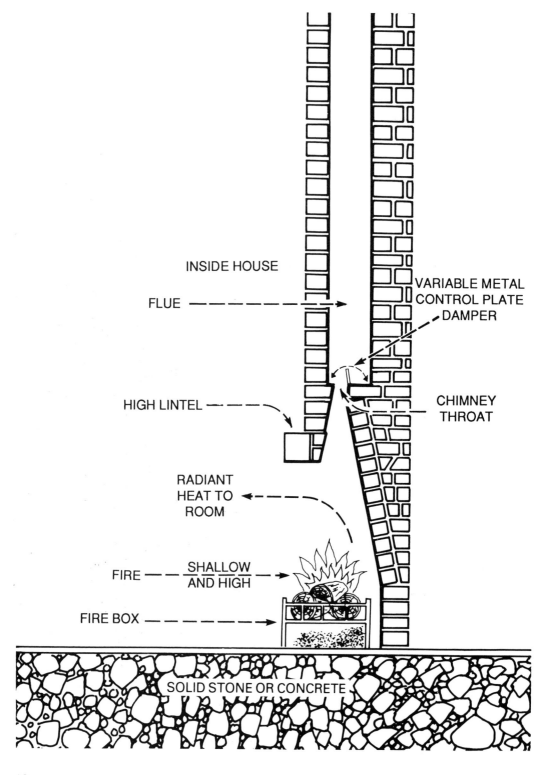

INSIDE HOUSE

FLUE

VARIABLE METAL
CONTROL PLATE
DAMPER

HIGH LINTEL

CHIMNEY
THROAT

RADIANT
HEAT TO
ROOM

FIRE — SHALLOW
AND HIGH

FIRE BOX

SOLID STONE OR CONCRETE

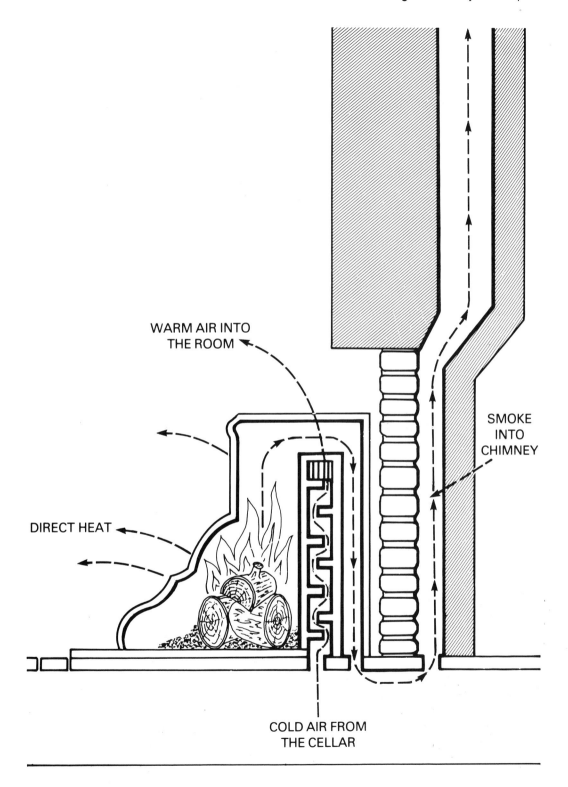

Fig 3 The Pennsylvania fireplace

WARM AIR INTO
THE ROOM

SMOKE
INTO
CHIMNEY

DIRECT HEAT

COLD AIR FROM
THE CELLAR

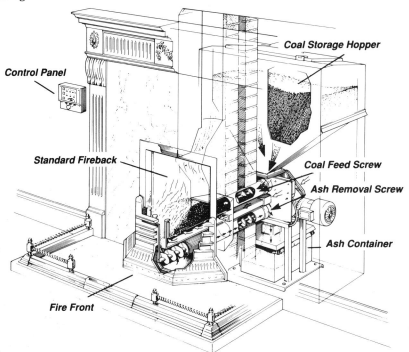

Fig 4 The Charnwood Fireflow

warmed, this rose and through a louvre at the top of the stove chamber was directed into the room, adding further warmth without draught. Then, as in Prince Rupert's design, the fire-gas was directed down to the rear side of the sealed baffle into the base of the chimney flue. In some versions of the design, Franklin incorporated a sliding metal plate that could control the rate at which hot fire-gas rose up the chimney. This additionally warmed the structure of the chimney and wall, creating a heat store which distributed further heat into the house. With character-istic generosity, Franklin refused to patent this design, making it freely available to everyone. Consequently, versions of it are still made in the USA, in Europe and the UK. Although some stoves are marketed under the name 'Franklin' they have no connection with Benjamin Franklin's designs.

The Charnwood Fireflow

Automated equipment has become a feature of many central heating systems, but has not previously been applied to the traditional open fire. A unique sensor-controlled open fire is now manufactured by Charnwood

Stoves on the Isle of Wight (see Useful Addresses).

To the casual gaze the Fireflow is a conventional living-room fire. But two items indicate technical advancement. Beside the fireplace (see illustration above) is a small, wall-mounted control box. It combines with a hand-held, infra-red remote control regulator. Built-in sensors co-ordinate fuel supply, fan-assisted air flow and ash removal. When a hot burn is required all three are increased proportionately, and vice-versa for 'slum-bering'.

Installation is relatively easy. The unit fits into a standard 16in fireplace. It penetrates the wall so that there is easy access to the electro-mechanical components for con-venient maintenance and adjustment.

Fuel, generally Coalflow Pearls or Anthracite beans, is delivered directly into a vitreous-enamelled hopper – capacity 175kg (367.5lb). Under normal use this should last for ten to fourteen days. Fuel is screwed into the fire, while ash is withdrawn to a container where it is cool enough to be sealed directly into a plastic bag. Once alight, the fire will continue to burn unattended, to a pre-selected temperature for as long as the fuel lasts. Relighting is no more difficult than for any other open, solid fuel fire.

2 Analysing the Problem

Placing the fire

When examining the best place for the stove or grate, the assumption at this stage will be that your house has no form of hearth or chimney. The analysis of the problem will be on the premise of heat efficiency alone, excluding all other factors. Since there is no hard and fast solution to the problem of siting the fire, the following are guidelines to help the householder find his own answer.

To retain as much as possible of the fire's heat output inside the house, the placing of the stove on any outside wall should be avoided. A proportion, and with certain types of fire, a very large proportion, of the generated heat will soak into the wall and, thereby, escape to the open air and be wasted.

A compromise location in a corner, at the junction of an inner and outer wall, is similarly best avoided, if for no better reason than such a position limits the number of persons who can comfortably sit close to the fire.

For the greatest heat retention, the fire should be placed as close as possible to the centre of the house and at the lowest practicable level. If you like to sit beside the fire, then clearly this rules out a basement or cellar location, despite the decided advantages this has in the matter of heat distribution. In addition, there are local authority building regulations that impose criteria which will be examined later. But purely in the name of heating efficiency, to use the house as a vast insulator that stores heat mainly in its walls as does a storage heater, then a fire placing on an inner wall as far away from the exterior is the best.

However, in most houses there are impediments to placing a stove in its best working position. Apart from the householder's personal preferences, they stem from the style of the house itself. Up to now it has been assumed that the hearthless or stoveless house in question is detached, but semi-detached and terraced homes pose their own problems.

Most semi-detached houses have a staircase

Photo 1 A good example of a centrally placed free-standing stove with exposed insulated metal flue

15

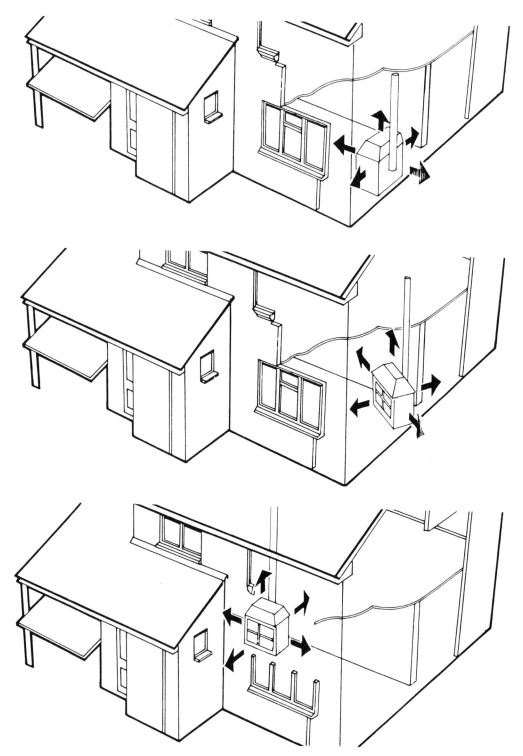

Fig 5 Siting of fires. *Top*: heat escapes through outside wall *Centre:* corner location – limited access
Bottom: best location – centre of room

rising up from a hallway or from a living-room. In either case this would prevent the stove from being placed centrally in the house and the interconnecting walls of the downstairs rooms would be difficult to work around. In any case, few housewives would sanction a flue-pipe rising vertically through the living area. In addition, there are limitations on such an installation imposed by building regulations (see pp 92 and 98).

The same considerations would generally apply to a terraced house. Even the modern open-plan style of terraced house needs enough structural members internally to make such a stove placing very costly and awkward. With both semi-detached and terraced houses, to place a stove or hearth against a common wall would generously bestow a free flow of heat to your neighbours.

None the less, compromise solutions are possible. One, for example, concerns the large room that has been created by knocking down the dividing wall between two small rooms. Normally, two doors remain for entering the one room. By closing off one door permanently, a free-standing stove or a hearth could be sited in the space taken by the doorway.

With the chimney checked, and all obstructions removed, the way is now clear to prepare a place for the fire. The following is a simple check-list to be worked through:

1 Is there a constructional hearth of the required thickness and surface area, made of acceptable non-burnable material? (See pp 85–6, 88, 96.)

2 If one is desired, is there a decorative or superimposed hearth? (See pp 85, 87.)

3 Is there a back hearth, ie a non-burnable surface of the required dimensions on which the fire may rest directly or on which a metal grate may be placed? (See pp 56, 85–6, 88.)

4 Is there a fireback of the required material and dimensions? Moulded firebacks made of fire-clay can be purchased from builders' merchants, stove shops or fireplace manufacturers.

These requirements satisfied, some type of open or closed fire can be installed at once. The opportunity can be taken to include one of the hundreds of decorative fireplace surrounds on offer.

Flow Charts

For a fire to work well, three criteria must be satisfied:

1 Air must flow into it.
2 Heat must radiate from it.
3 Hot fire-gas must escape from it.

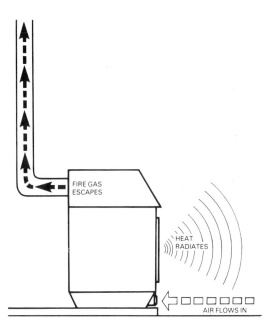

FIRE GAS ESCAPES

HEAT RADIATES

AIR FLOWS IN

Fig 6

In order to calculate the best position for your fire, an approximate layout of the ground floor should be drawn on a sheet of graph paper. Mark on it all doors, windows and ventilators (especially permanent ventilating bricks in the wall and any other connections to the exterior).

Prepare a similar sheet for the first floor and a page for each additional floor. Include a layout for the basement or cellar if you have either. Finally, construct a plan for the attic.

On the ground-floor plan, imagine the fire to be in the position you have chosen for it. Try to visualise where its supply of fresh air will come from. Is there an adequate supply?

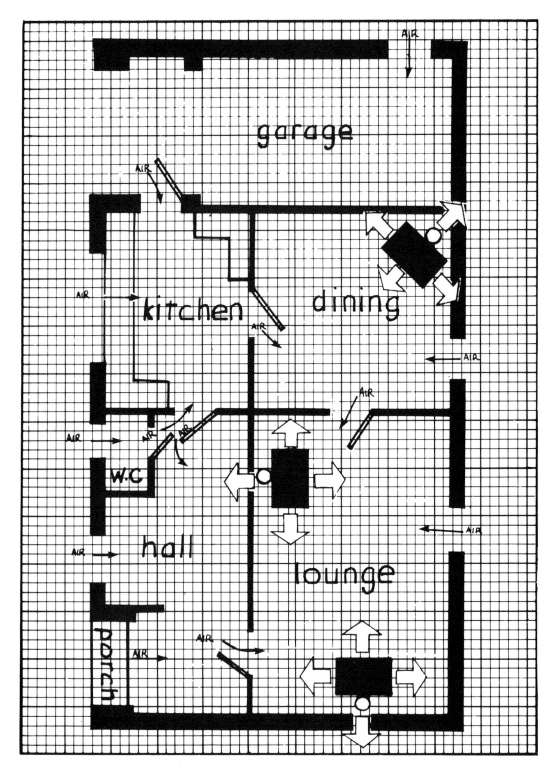

Fig 7 An example of a flow chart

Might it be likely to create unpleasant draughts?

Radiant heat will come from the fire in more or less straight lines, not only from the burning fire itself, but also from the hot sides and top of the stove. You can easily show on your chart the limits of its distribution.

The heat which radiates from the stove, on all its sides, will warm the air which rises. Where will it rise to? How may warm air reach the first floor and other floors above? How effective will your attic or loft be in preventing the escape of what heat remains in the air to the outside?

Draw the fire in a different position and construct another set of flow charts. Compare the results, and repeat as necessary, until you have found a position for your fire that seems to satisfy all its working requirements as well as those of your own home comfort.

When you have decided upon the most satisfactory position for your fire, it is necessary to consider the flow of cold air, for when hot fire-gas is exhausted from the chimney it needs to be replaced by fresh air flowing into the room in which the fire is placed. If this does not happen a partial vacuum is created. This stops the fire smoke escaping from the chimney and the fire will not burn well.

If the fire design you have chosen takes its air from above floor level then it is necessary to check that there is some source of ventilation into the room through which replacement air can flow. This air must be vented in such a way that it does not create cold draughts.

Check the fit of windows and doors to determine the degree to which they will allow air to pass, into the heated room. Note the position of any air-bricks built into the walls and see that they are not obstructed by curtains or furniture.

Should you have chosen a fire that takes its air from below floor level, or from the exterior (see pp 54, 65–6), this will by pass the living-room draught problem.

A similar check must be made of the underfloor space to make sure that it has adequate ventilation and that air-bricks and the honeycomb of 'sleeper' walls (ie separating walls) are clear of obstruction. In certain designs the underfloor air supply (either from inside the house or from the exterior) is an integral part of the design and the constructional hearth on which it stands (see pp 66–8, 75–9).

Calculating Heat Requirements

It is a widely held fallacy that there is some precise way of determining the heat requirement in a house. A moment's thought will show this to be unreal.

Should the external temperature fall to 10°C (50°F), the heat requirement to sustain a given comfortable temperature in a particular room may double. In addition, the cooling

Fig 8 Underfloor air supply

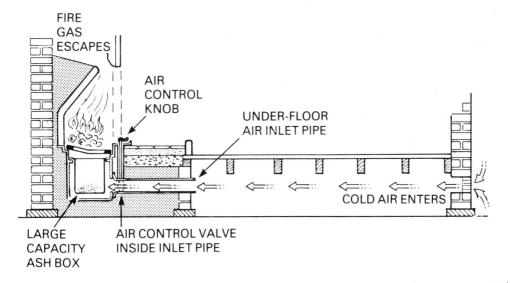

FIRE GAS ESCAPES

AIR CONTROL KNOB

UNDER-FLOOR AIR INLET PIPE

COLD AIR ENTERS

LARGE CAPACITY ASH BOX

AIR CONTROL VALVE INSIDE INLET PIPE

Photo 2 A Centro Bell fireplace centrally placed in a living room

effect of winds of differing strengths and temperatures, coming from various directions, will also alter this requirement. Add to this the effects of changing atmospheric humidity and pressure, and the calculation begins to seem daunting. Compound this with the variables in performance of any given heating appliance and the calculation appears to be beyond reasonable achievement. There are marked variations in heat output depending on the type of fuel in use. Coal has double the output, volume for volume, on an average supply of wood logs.

The ratings attached to stove models in showrooms (registered in kilowatts or British thermal units per hour) are of very little help in making the decision whether a particular stove model will heat a room or house of known dimensions. The same heat output can come from a small stove working flat out, or from a much larger design burning fuel at no more than tick-over or idling rate.

Should the external temperature suddenly drop, the smaller stove will have no reserve capacity to deal with this. Should. the external temperature rise, it may not be possible to damp down the larger model's heat output to a comfortable level and prevent the build up of condensates in the chimney flue.The calculation may need to include whether a stove can heat properly the room in which it stands, as well as serving several radiators and supplying domestic hot water.

There is, however, a rule of thumb method that experience has shown to be a reliable guide. Measure in feet the room in which the stove is to be installed. For adequate performance under average conditions and with additional capacity to supply other services or to cope with extreme conditions, the fire-chamber of the stove should have the same dimensions in inches as the room has in feet. For example, a living-room may be 20ft long,15ft wide and 10ft high – a total of 3,000ft³.The stove fire-chamber should measure no less than approximately 20in long, 15in wide or deep and 10in high – 3,000in³ in total.

Hot Air

In planning where to place a stove in a hearthless home, you must consider the problems of heat distribution as well as those of direct heating. Central heating is now as standardised a requirement in the modern home as mains water, electricity and drainage. The careful placing of the stove, resulting from a study of the heat flow chart, has already laid the foundation for this to be implemented.

Heat distribution throughout the house can

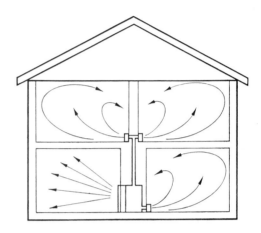

Fig 9 Ducted warm air heating

be achieved by either hot air or hot water. Here, we consider the first of these systems.

The Romans centrally heated their homes by ducting hot air beneath their main floors. Today, in North America, most homes are heated centrally by hot air. The heater is generally placed in the basement or cellar, although in some houses the heater is a wall-mounted, automatic unit. American-style open-plan houses allow warm air to circulate freely. Slots cut in the floor/ceiling between each storey open the way for it to rise up through the house.

Wood is the commonest structural material in North American houses and is an incomparably better insulator than brick. Consequently, in this country we must pay more attention to house insulation. Furthermore, fewer UK households are constructed to a full open-plan and their design allows little circulation of warm air around the house.

None the less, in appropriate circumstances, hot-air central heating can be efficient and cheap, requiring less physical installation than water. Although ducts are often employed to guide the air through the house, these are not entirely necessary, being more of a concession to the traditional design of our homes than to efficiency.

Hot Water

Most houses in the UK consist of a number of separate rooms which are isolated from each other. This is particularly true of houses built before 1939 or in the years immediately after 1945. The tendency today is for the ground floor to be wholly or partially open-plan, with the first floor bedrooms remaining as individual units. This layout is best centrally heated by circulating hot water to one or more radiators in each room. Undoubtedly, the installation costs will probably be higher than those for hot air, but that cannot be avoided. To secure the best operational efficiency bestows a long-term advantage

Many conflicting claims are made for the heating outputs of different designs of radiators. However, rule-of-thumb decisions as to the number of radiators required for adequate home heating and their best placings, can be determined with relative ease and simplicity.

It can be assumed that the required average background temperature in a room not occupied full-time is about 18°C (65°F). (Living-rooms should not fall below 21°C (70°F) for comfort.) A heat flow chart, constructed on the principles described on pp 17–22 will indicate where radiators should be placed in each room (a typical arrangement is illustrated on p 18).

While some types of radiator have a marginal working advantage over others, as a general rule it can be accepted that there should be roughly a 25:1 ratio between the surface area of the radiator (measured on one side) and the surface area of the room it is heating. Stated simply, if the equivalent of twenty-five radiators can be laid flat on the floor of the room, then one radiator of that size will sustain an average temperature of 18°C (65°F) (assuming that the house is reasonably well constructed and insulated). Of course, if the external temperature falls abnormally low, or rises to an unseasonally high level, the room temperature will rise or fall accordingly.

There can be no doubt that for British homes of traditional design, hot-water central heating has the advantage over hot air. It is compatible with most heating systems (solid fuel, gas, oil, electricity, wood). In addition, with only a nominal increase in the consumption of fuel, it can supply domestic hot water.

Radiators

It is virtually outside the range of this book to deal fully with central-heating systems although there are many such guides available. The types of stove or boiler to which hot-water pipes can be connected have been described and a sample hot-air system examined (see p 21). However, to make the chain of connection complete, a few of the many models now available are described.

Clyde Combustions Ltd (see Useful Addresses) make three ranges of traditional steel column and cast-iron column radiators. In addition, they produce Stabulo steel-column radiators in two styles for low, medium- and high-pressure hot-water systems.

Sensotherm Superads are made in Italy and subjected to German DIN performance testing. They are light in weight and because their water content is low, heat pick up is rapid. The finish is a durable white stove enamel. Because they are made of extruded aluminium, a wider than usual variety of shapes and sizes is available.

Zehnder radiators are constructed from 1.5mm ($\frac{1}{20}$in) sheet or tubular steel. A feature of their design is the absence of cover plates, sharp corners or edges. There are over six thousand shapes and sizes from which to choose.

Heat Insulation

There are two routes, primarily, by which heat can escape from a house: horizontally, out through the walls, and vertically, rising up through the house to leak from the roof.

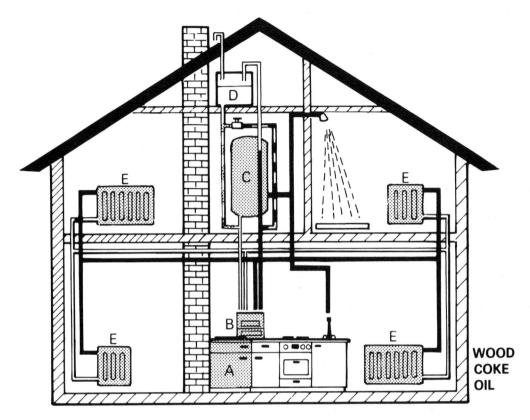

WOOD
COKE
OIL

Analysing the problem

It is clear, therefore, that house walls should provide some degree of heat insulation. In older homes, solid brick walls are quite effective. Wooden walls are very good insulators, as are traditional solid stone walls. Slate is a moderately good insulator, except that it offers a horizontal path between the layers to the passage of moisture. Modern cavity walls trap heat successfully as the air between the two brick skins is a poor conductor of heat. This insulation can be improved by filling the cavity with some non-heat-conducting substance, although care must be taken that this does not, thereby, supply a flow path for damp (see p 88).

The techniques for lining and insulating the roof are by now much simplified and well understood.

There is another aspect of heat insulation imposed by building regulations, namely, that a minimum air gap must exist between a stove and surrounding combustible material (the photograph p 25 shows what these are).

Fig 10 Typical hot-water system. **A.** Central cooking system. **B.** Four-way mixing valve with circulating pump. **C.** Domestic hot water cylinder.**D.** Expansion tank. **E.** Radiators

Where it is not possible to arrange a large enough air gap, a heat shield can be inserted. One of the simplest and cheapest comes from Canada, consisting of a metal frame in which are inserted ordinary wall-tiles. Individual decorative designs can be created to match the surroundings.

Another form of heat insulation that is given relatively little attention in the UK, even when the opportunity to install it exists, is the creation of a 'shelter belt'. It is widely acknowledged in North America where tests have shown that more heat can be contained within the house by creating a shelter belt than by all other means put together.

A shelter belt is a line of trees planted across the direction of the prevailing wind (see Fig 11). Although in North America, with its endless flat plains, wind direction is more constant than it is in the UK, none the

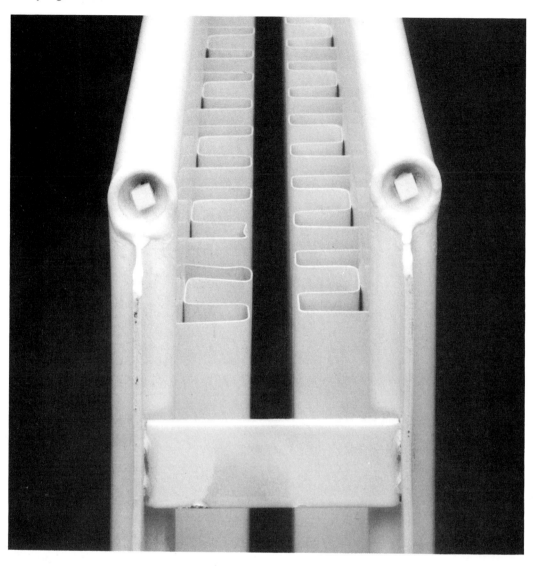

Photo 3 The Myson round top radiator

Photo 4 Sensotherm radiators

Photo 5 Zehnder radiator

less, even here it can be presumed that winds come from the west or south-west more often than from any other direction.

A shelter belt is usually composed of fast-growing conifers. These need to be 15–30m (50–100ft) from the house and 7–9m (25–30ft) tall. It is, therefore, a long-term project to create a shelter belt and presumes enough open land surrounding the house. It can, however, save hundreds of pounds on a winter heating bill and, once in place, requires little attention

Photo 6 Finrad Convectorad 105

Photo 7 An 'illegal' stove installation. There is no constructional hearth – as required by building regulations – and insufficient clearance between the back of the stove case and the house wall

25

and will last the life of the trees.

While detailed consideration is generally given to loft insulation, the same emphasis is not given to loft ventilation, although it is of matching importance. Any localised build up of heat can easily damage insulating materials, especially those based on glass-fibre whose temperature should never exceed 250°C (480°F).

As an alternative to laying fibrous roof insulation,contractors can pour this substance from pipes. The technique is useful where awkward volumes with low headroom have to be insulated.

External wall insulation is now available for houses where any other technique would be difficult or impossible. It consists of a cladding of rigid flame-retardant polystyrene panels laid on a bed of high adhesive mortar and coated with a special polymer mortar incorporating a reinforcing glass-fibre mesh. The external finish is a self-coloured, textured mortar. Because this method changes the external appearance of a building, it is not advised for homes with a period look.

Ventilation Units

When the traditional British house is double-glazed and draught-proofed, this often leads to a lack of adequate air movement, particularly in the living-room with a coal fire which requires a good supply of oxygen. One solution is to install ventilation units on the walls between rooms so that air can be drawn in from the outside. For example, a unit might be fitted in the wall between a living-room and the kitchen where windows, doors or vents open to let in fresh air.

Among a variety of models, two ventilation units are typical. They ventilate without creating draughts.

Draught Master is a one-way air inlet, controlled by a hinged flap. Air can flow into a room through it, but cannot escape back. Its return path to the exterior is through the fire which, thereby, burns more strongly.

The Reclaire is somewhat more elaborate. It introduces fresh air into a room without losing all the heat of the old, stale air, which it replaces. This is accomplished through a heat exchanger. The heat of the old air is used to warm the cold fresh air before it circulates into the living space. Electricity is required to drive the operating fans, but no additional electricity is used to heat the incoming air.

Fig 11 Shelter belt

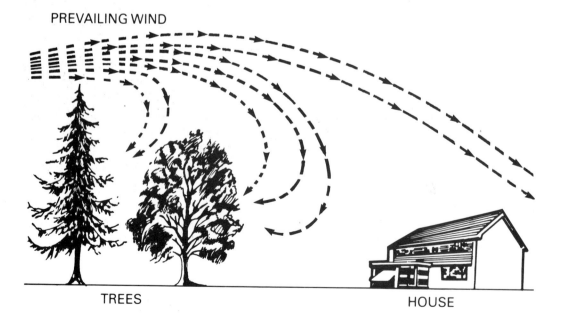

PREVAILING WIND

TREES

HOUSE

Photo 8 Alternative internal house insulation is available using drylining material

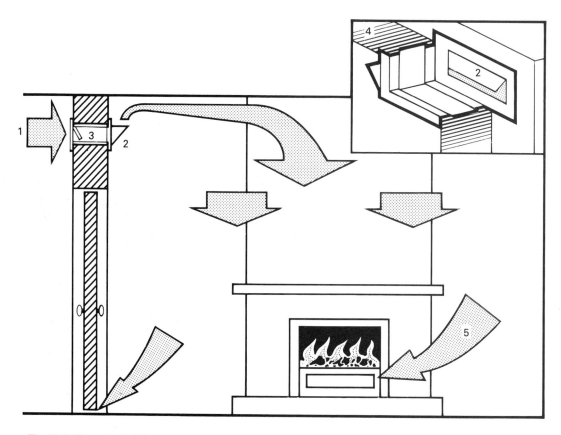

Fig 12 1 Clean air in **2** Draughtmaster **3** One-way
hinged flap **4** Equal pressure counteracts draughts **5**
Adequate air gives bright burning fires

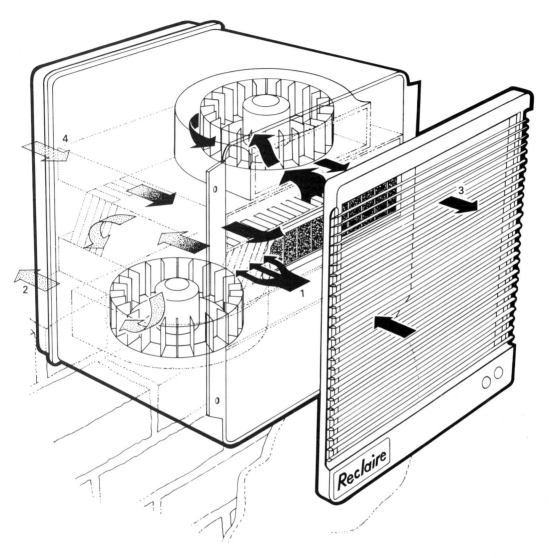

Fig 13 1 Stale air enters Reclaire **2** Stale, cool indoor air exhausted to outside **3** Fresh, heated air enters room **4** Outside air enters at low temperature

3 Fuels

Wood

More than any other fuel, the use of wood demands considerable preparation and provision.

All over the UK there is evidence of trees being planted, both by the Forestry Commission and private owners, to replace those that are cut down. One stimulus is the assurance investors now enjoy that over a ten-year period they can expect a better return on their capital from forestry than from the average industrial investment. Since 1946 there has been a steady increase each year in the area of trees planted.

Yet often, in well-wooded districts, there is claimed to be a shortage of wood fuel. Generally. the cause is not so much one of shortage but of the means of commercially distributing it. In such circumstances, householders with wood-burning appliances must make their own provision. Agreements can be made and permits secured to cut and take the non-commercial remnants of other wood-marketing activity. Approaches to the district officer of the Forestry Commission, woodland estate managers, local saw-mills or industries that use quantities of wood will often produce abundant supplies.

Measured by weight or volume, wood has only half the heat potential of coal. In addition, wood is delivered in volumetric loads, about a half of which consists of air gaps. Therefore, to be competitive, wood must cost no more than a quarter of the comparable price of coal.

Of vital importance is the availability, within a reasonable distance, of a reliable supply of wood fuel at a competitive price. Ideally, the wood should be available throughout the year, although many suppliers operate on a seasonal basis.

Once a good supply of wood has been obtained it is important to remember that burning sap-wet wood produces a feeble heat and risks the possibility of a chimney fire. Before cut wood can be used as a fuel, there-fore, it must be air-dried for a minimum of six months, and longer if possible.

The purpose of air-drying is to remove the sap. It is mistakenly thought that wood is air-dried as a protection against rain damp, but this is not so. In properly matured wood its natural resins prevent the penetration of surface wetness. Being merely a surface condition, rain damp dries almost as quickly as it occurs.

Sap wetness imposes two acute penalties. First, before the wood can burn the sap must be driven off. This takes up at least half the wood's potential heat output and results in a poor fire.

Secondly, because of its low working temperature, a sap-wet fire will result in only mildly warm fire-gas rising up the chimney flue. At that low temperature layers of wood tar will be precipitated on the flue's inner wall. This will gradually close the flue, further reducing the fire's effective performance. Eventually, enough mild heat will be trapped to ignite the wood tar. The consequent chimney fire will probably cause severe damage to the chimney, if not the rest of the roof and house.

That said, wood is probably the easiest solid fuel to burn as it makes the least demands on the home-heating system. In its simplest form it needs only a flat surface, access to air and to be placed beneath a chimney flue.

If the wood fire is to be within a recess (see p 87), it should be wide enough to accommodate logs of a reasonable length when laid sideways (ie about 600mm (24in)) – a few millimetres either way is not important. In the unlikely, but not entirely impractical, event that the fire is not within a recess but free-standing, these same general provisions apply.

There should be a raised lip along the front edge of the burning surface so that accumulations of wood-ash can be removed from time to time with a small hand shovel. The deeper the lip, the more ash that can be conveniently

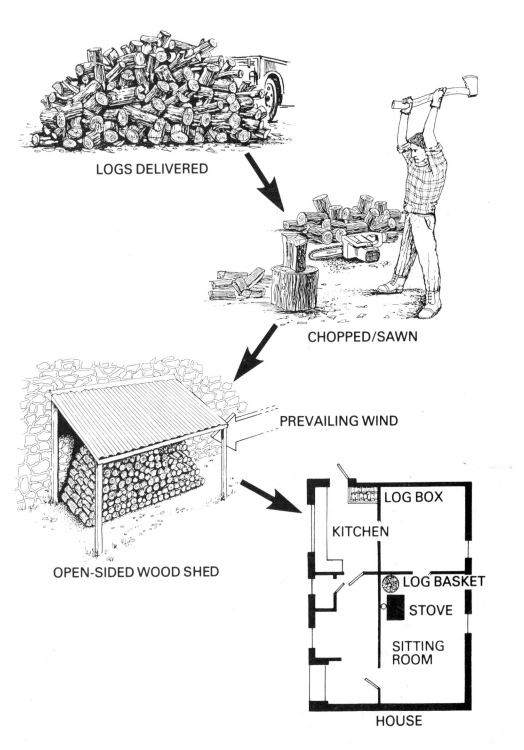

LOGS DELIVERED

CHOPPED/SAWN

PREVAILING WIND

OPEN-SIDED WOOD SHED

LOG BOX

KITCHEN

LOG BASKET

STOVE

SITTING ROOM

HOUSE

Fig 14 Wood fuel store

contained and less frequently will the ash have to be cleared away. However, the lip should not be so deep that it becomes awkward to remove the ash. Probably a depth of 50-75mm (2-3in) would be, on average, the most convenient. With this capacity of wood-ash store, burning the fire for several hours daily, it should not be necessary to remove the ash more than once every ten to fourteen days.

A simple wood fire of this type will burn well, although inefficiently, as most of its heat will escape up the chimney. It can easily be ignited by laying screws of paper across its base. Over these place wood kindling (twigs, etc) and small dry wood pieces. As soon as the fire takes hold it can be built up with larger logs until a good blaze is established. Alternatively, a wigwam of wood pieces can be built around one or two solid paraffin wax fire-lighters (see illustration on p 38).

When lighting a closed stove all air vents (top and bottom) should be wide open. With an open fire, if there is a chimney vent, this too should be fully opened.

As with all solid fuels, a wood fire chimney should be swept a least once every year and more frequently if used heavily.

If you decide to install a wood-burning stove, you should consider whether there is adequate storage capacity that is readily accessible outside the house. It should be possible to store about a year's supply of wood, or at least enough to heat the house throughout the winter.

A wood store should not be totally enclosed as this can cause the wood to sweat. An open-sided shelter with, preferably, a half wall on the side facing the prevailing wind (probably the west or south-west) is the best.

For a winter season's supply for a three-bedroomed house, the storage capacity should be just under 70M^3 (2,000ft^3) ie about the size of a large single-car garage. There should be enough space around the wood store for chopping and sawing, and it should be far enough away from any other building (especially neighbours' houses) so that wood bits and sawdust do not create a nuisance.

Check that there is enough room for a lorry to unload logs. Deliveries of air-dried logs should be taken all through the summer. Chop and saw these to sizes convenient for your stove and stack them under the shelter

so that you start the winter with a full supply. During the winter, replace the store with fresh logs as the old ones are used. Thereby, your wood fuel should always be fully air dried.

Immediately inside the house there should be sufficient space for a wood box, large enough to hold two or three days' supply. This is to avoid having to forage for wood outside during short periods of bad weather.

A log basket large enough to hold an evening's supply should stand beside the stove or fireplace, The flooring on your route from the wood box to the basket should be hard-wearing as wood bits are inevitably lost when logs are transferred.

If these criteria can be satisfied, your house will be suitable for heating with wood fuel.

Wood-based Fuels and Peat

To utilise the waste wood from forestry and industrial working, a variety of wood-based processed fuels have come on the market in the UK. There is little point in listing their names as few are nationally distributed. However, despite variations in size, colour and texture, they are all based on two manu-facturing methods.

In the first, wood is broken down to any size from small chips to dust. A bonding agent is added and the resulting fuel is secured by low-pressure moulding. The disadvantage of fuels made by this technique is that when their temperature is raised to that at which combustion occurs, the bond either ignites or liquefies and the fuel falls apart into its constituent parts. Lacking the essential homogeneity for a controlled burn rate, such fuels tend to be uncertain in performance, often burning at an excessive rate with wasteful generation of heat, or choking and going out.

The second process is more expensive to achieve but results in a more controllable fuel. Wood is reduced to chips and subjected to a very high pressure which generates heat and plasticises the wood's natural resins. When the pressure is suddenly released these resins harden, holding the wood in any shape imposed by the press.

Fuels of this type are an acceptable alterna-tive to natural wood. They are, however, more expensive, often being sold at prices marginally lower than that of coal, but they

are convenient, clean, require no chopping and sawing and produce little ash.

It is possible to identify the fuels made by these two processes by their 'feel'. The high-pressure wood fuels tend to be much more dense, ie they feel heavier and more compacted than the low-pressure fuels.

Natural charcoal and its processed forms are also wood-based fuels. They are, in effect, the highest grade of wood fuel and would be acceptable as an ordinary domestic fuel were it not for the artificially high prices at which they are sold in Britain, particularly for the barbecue market.

Peat and processed peat blocks are also acceptable as domestic fuels, although price is an inhibitant. They usually require strong draughting in the stove or fireplace for even, slow burning. Tests have established that overnight burning is practicable.

Other alternative fuels, such as small presses for moulding wet newspaper into fuel briquettes, are available. Experimental use has shown them to be expensive, inconvenient and poor performers in heat generation (see p 34 for comparative performance figures).

Photo 9 The Austrian Pusch cutter-splitter reduces logs to workable size for domestic fuelling

Photo 10 Processed Heatlogs burning in a Jetmaster fire-place in the lounge bar of The Rising Sun, Knapp, Somerset

Fig 15
Comparative heating costs

May 1991 **United Kingdom Regional Summary**
Cost of space and water heating for an average three bedroom house £[4]

Fuel	Type of heating system	South east	South west and Wales	Midland	Northern England	Scotland	Northern Ireland
Housecoal Gp B[1]	Open fire with back boiler, radiators & DHW cylinder	476	415	425	402	446	502
Anthracite Nuts[2]	Room heater with backboiler, radiators & DHW cylinder	526	454	460	530	526	513
Housewarm singles	Room heater with backboiler, radiators & DHW cylinder	–	–	386	387	–	–
Anthracite grains	Gravity feed boiler, radiators & DHW cylinder	445	398	401	399	467	447
Coalflow pearls	Coalflow underfeed boiler radiators & DHW cylinder	440	395	419	427	437	437
Electricity standard	Electric radiators DHW cylinder with immersion heater	1215	1218	1299	1346	1265	1287
Economy 7[3]	Storage heaters & electric fire, DHW cylinder with IMM heater	570	548	588	605	645	537
Gas credit tariff	Boiler, radiators & DHW cylinder	490	470	502	522	540	–
	Condensing boiler, radiators & DHW cylinder	414	398	423	440	455	–
LPG propane (bulk)	Boiler, radiators & DHW cylinder	746	714	764	797	825	777
	Condensing boiler, radiators & DHW cylinder	625	598	639	666	690	652
Heating Oil	Boiler, radiators & DHW cylinder	390	375	398	414	445	425
	Condensing boiler, radiators & DHW cylinder	327	315	334	346	372	355

Space heating for an average sized room £[5]

Fuel	Type of heating system	South east	South west and Wales	Midland	Northern England	Scotland	Northern Ireland
Housecoal Gp B	Open fire	174	151	158	152	170	187
Coalite	Open fire	210	190	169	176	199	213
Anthracite nuts	Closed room heater	111	97	100	114	115	111
Electricity standard	Electric fire	220	218	236	247	236	237
economy 7[3]	Single storage heater & electric fire	117	110	120	123	137	112
Gas credit tariff	Radiant/convective fire	146	141	149	154	159	–
	Wall heater	132	128	134	138	143	–
	Decorative effect open fire	235	224	241	252	263	–
LPG Propane (cylinder)	Radiant/convective fire	265	249	273	288	304	312
	Decorative effect closed front fire	265	249	273	288	304	312
	Decorative effect open fire	533	500	550	584	617	633
LPG Butane (cylinder)	Portable heater	171	160	177	188	199	149

Notes
(1) Northern Ireland fuel is English Housecoal.
(2) Northern England fuel is Sunbrite Coke.
(3) Assumed 90% of use at off peak rate, 95% Northern Ireland.
(4) Space heating 12,100 kWh to 15, 200 kWh depending on region. Water heating 2,500 kWh.
(5) Space heating 2800 kWh to 3500 kWh depending on region.
(6) Electricity and Gas standing charges, LPG cylinder rental, cost of maintenance and running circulating pump included as required.

Sutherland Associates, Building Services and Energy Consultants ©

A

C

Photos 11–14 (a) A skip load of broken wood is delivered; (b) The wood is crushed and compressed at great pressure; (c) Processed logs travel along the conveyor belt, and (d) are bagged ready for delivery

B

D

Manufactured Smokeless Fuels

The burning performance of coal can be improved by various manufacturing processes. The general characteristics of the resulting fuels is that they are more uniform in size than natural coal, are virtually soot-less, clean to handle and leave little ash residue; and they burn with an even red heat with little flame, at a steady rate and relatively slowly, giving a regular heat output.

Coke is the oldest of these coal-derived fuels and is made by heating coal in a sealed oven to a temperature of 1,000°C (1,830°F). This results in the volatile substances being driven off in the form of thick brown smoke, from which is extracted tar, sulphur, ammonia and benzole. Coke has about a third more heating potential than coal and performs well in both open and closed stoves.

Sunbrite is made by a similar process, except that the coal is first crushed and blended. It is not suitable for open fires (except those with underfloor draughting).

Phurnacite is manufactured by the National Coal Board at Caerphilly in South Wales. Welsh dry steam coal and anthracite are ground down to fine particles which are bound with pitch and moulded into egg-shaped pieces (ovoids). These are then heated in retorts to drive off most of the volatile matter. Phurnacite is suitable for most domestic closed stoves.

Multi-heat, also manufactured by the NCB, is made from small anthracite (duff), which is mixed with pitch, creosote and coking coal. This mixture is pressed into ovoids and then passed through a sand bed where it is heated to nearly 400°C (750°F). At this heat most of the smoke-producing volatile substances are driven off. Finally, the briquettes are water sprayed to remove any dust. This fuel's performance is similar to Phurnacite, but because it has about double the volatile content (10 per cent as compared with 5 per cent) and a higher heating potential, it should not be used in hopper-fed appliances or those with narrow flues (ie heat storage cookers). Coalite is made from small, medium and weakly coking coals, blended and heated in vertical retorts, from which air is excluded, to a temperature of 630°C (1,170°F). The carbonised fuel is then discharged into sealed chambers where it is cooled for almost four hours in an air-free atmosphere. The fuel comes in three sizes: coalite, nuts and peas.

Rexco is a coke-type fuel made from washed small cobble or nut-sized coal. This is heated to between 700°C and 800°C (1,290° and 1,470°F) in large cylindrical vertical retorts which are heated internally by hot gases being drawn downwards through the coal. Three grades are produced: Openfire, Nuts and Rexcobrite. Ovoids are also made from the waste dust of the main process.

Roomheat is made from crushed coal by a new process pioneered by the National Coal Board. When crushed, the coal is carbonised in a special retort known as a fluidiser. After twenty minutes at a temperature of 430°C (806°F) the coal is converted to char, which is then formed into solid briquettes by passing through a large mangle-type press. Alternatively, the char can be fed through an extrusion press producing a continuous tube of fuel. In this form it is known as Homefire. Coal treated in this manner responds as if it were a liquid and this is identified as the 'fluidised bed' process

New consolidated legislation extends authorisation to all the fuels listed below for use in Smoke Control Areas in any part of Great Britain. All are briquettes, unless stated otherwise, listed by manufacturer and fuel:

Agglonord, France – Anthracine N20, Anthranor, Antrex;

AIMCOR, Netherlands – Pureheat ovoids (petroleum coke, not for domestic use);

Alfred McAlpine – Flamelite Pellets;

Association Co-operative Zelandaise de Carbonisation, Netherlands – Dutch (Sluiskil) Coke Doubles (coke);

Coalite Products – Coalite (coals, nuts, peas);

CPL–Ancit, Ancit 40, Beacon Beans (coke), Homefire, Phurnacite, Sunbrite (coke);

Fritz Selbmann, Germany – Thermaglow;

Greystone Heating – Centurion;

Les Combustibles de Normandie, and La Société Rouennaise – Fireglo;

Maxibrite – Maxibrite;

Monckton Coke – Monckton Boiler Beans (coke), Sovereign, Sunbrite (coke);

Sophia-Jacoba – Extracite;

Photos 15–17 Typical samples of Welsh Dry Steam Coal (above left), Housecoal (left), and Phurnacite (above)

Taybrite – Clean Flame, New Taylor; Thermac Fuels – Supertherm, Thermac; Volkseigner Betrieb Gaskombinat – Thermobrite.

Coal

Coal was formed between 220 and 270 million years ago when much of the Earth's surface was covered with thick forests and swamps. Coal, in fact, is wood and vegetable matter that has decayed under pressure. Virtually any country which produced forests in the distant past will have seams of coal although many cannot be mined practicably.

Coal formation occurs progressively. In its early stages it results in peat which has a high (80 per cent) moisture content. Once this is driven off the resulting fibrous fuel burns well.

Lignite, or brown coal, is the first stage in the formation of fully mature coal. There is little fuel of this category in the UK, although it is mined and marketed extensively elsewhere, notably in Eastern Europe where it is one of the commonest domestic fuels.

Bituminous coal is a term embracing the lower grades of coal sold in Britain. It is not smokeless and cannot be burned in Smoke Control Zones.

Semi-bituminous coals are known as low volatile or dry steam coals. Many of these are graded as smokeless fuels.

Anthracite is the highest grade of coal and

Fig 16 Fire lighting – wood/coal

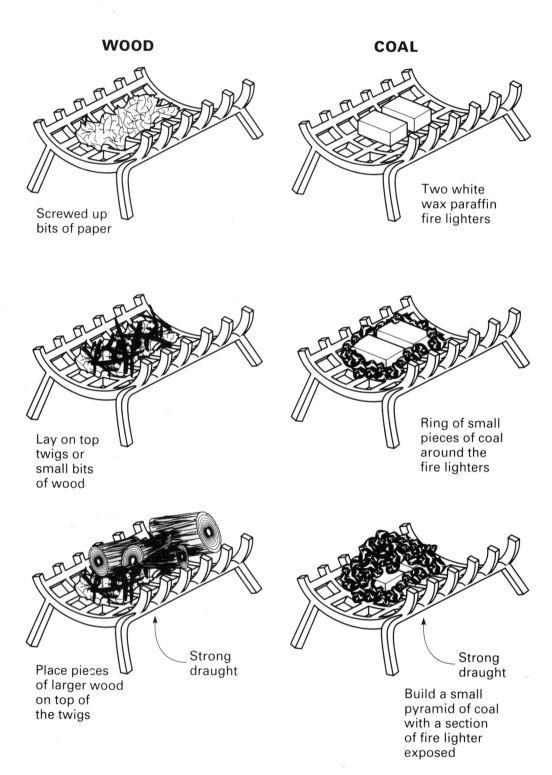

WOOD

COAL

Screwed up
bits of paper

Two white
wax paraffin
fire lighters

Lay on top
twigs or
small bits
of wood

Ring of small
pieces of coal
around the
fire lighters

Place pieces
of larger wood
on top of
the twigs

Strong
draught

Strong
draught

Build a small
pyramid of coal
with a section
of fire lighter
exposed

almost pure carbon. It has the highest heating value of all coals sold in Britain, is smokeless and produces very little ash. It is also the most expensive.

Coal is also graded by size. To some degree, these sizes overlap and the precise grading depends on the quality of the fuel being sized. The principal grades are:

Large coal	Minimum size 50mm (2in)
Large cobbles	75mm (3in) – 150mm (6in)
Small cobbles	50mm (2in) – 100mm (4in)
Trebles	50mm (2in) – 75mm (3in)
Doubles	25mm (1in) – 50mm (2in)
Singles	12mm ($\frac{1}{2}$in) – 25mm (1in)
Smalls	Below 25mm (1in)

Measured either by weight or volume, coal has about double the heat-producing potential of wood. Any fire uses oxygen at a rate that is roughly proportionate to its production of heat, so that a coal fire needs twice the oxygen supply of a wood fire of the same size. Equally, coal burns at a much higher temperature than wood.

It is necessary for air to be able to feed into a coal fire from any direction (ie from the sides, front, behind and from below). To achieve this the fire must be placed on a grate or in a fire-basket that will support it above the floor level of the hearth.

Poorer quality coal tends to light more readily than the best grades because it combusts at a lower temperature. Household coal should be ignited with all the air vents (top and bottom) wide open in a closed stove and with the chimney vent fully open in an open fire. Paper screws, twigs and kindling can be used, but the fire will take some nursing before it takes hold. A much easier technique is to employ two white wax paraffin fire-lighters (packets can be purchased in most supermarkets, ironmongers or hardware shops). Lay these flat on the bars of the fire-grate so that a strong draught can rise up past them. Place a ring of small coal pieces around them. Using these as a foundation, build a small pyramid of coal (see illustration). Leave an air gap so that a corner of one fire-lighter can be lit, then close this gap with a final piece of coal. As the flames strengthen and penetrate the air gaps, add additional pieces until the fire has taken a good hold. Again, all air vents should be

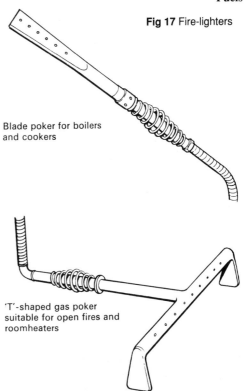

Fig 17 Fire-lighters

Blade poker for boilers and cookers

'T'-shaped gas poker suitable for open fires and roomheaters

Photo 18 The Grenadier electric fire-lighter (see Useful Addresses)

fully opened.

With open fireplaces, it was once the common practice to stretch a newspaper across the front of the hearth to improve the draught. This is not recommended, however, for the paper can suddenly ignite with a severe risk of the person concerned being burned.

A gas poker, consisting of a short pierced metal tube and using either piped or bottled gas, will ignite any coal fire in a few moments.

A more restrained method is to use an electric hot-air heater rather like a large hair dryer. The nozzle is inserted into the base of the coal in the grate. In a closed stove, the doors should be closed as far as possible. After a few moments the coal is heated to combustion level and spontaneously ignites. Once this happens, it is important to remove the heater at once.

Natural Smokeless Fuels

There are only two categories of naturally mined coal that can be burned legally in Smoke Control Zones: anthracite and dry steam coal.

Anthracite burns with a concentrated, long-lasting heat. Containing very little volatile substance, it is both smokeless and sootless. Unfortunately, because it ignites at a relatively high temperature, an anthracite fire is not an easy one to get started. Once alight, it requires a strong, steady draught. It burns slowly, with only a small flame.

Anthracite sold for domestic use (ie for hot-water boilers, room heaters and cookers) is graded in sizes that are often of only local application and additional to those already listed on p 39. They range upwards from grains, peas and beans to nuts and cobbles. Closed stoves offer the best opportunity for using anthracite efficiently. Few open fires can supply it with a strong enough draught.

Only about $2\frac{1}{2}$ million tonnes of anthracite are mined annually in the UK and further supplies have to be imported

Dry steam coal is also known as Welsh steam coal. Like anthracite, it is in limited supply. While categorised as a smokeless fuel, it has more volatile matter than anthracite and is correspondingly easier to ignite, although it still requires a strong draught. Domestic supplies are usually graded as small or large nuts.

As with anthracite, it is suitable for most domestic appliances (except open fires, gravity feed or automatic stoking units and heat storage cookers).

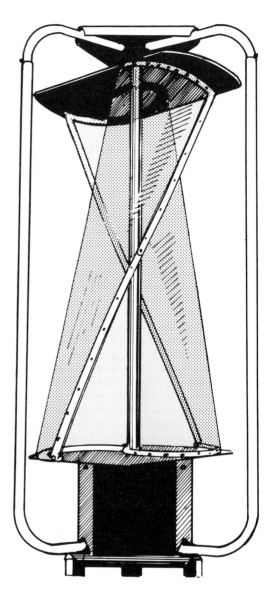

Fig 18 Wind generator

Electricity

Electricity is strictly an energy source and not a fuel – a term applied only to substances that generate heat by combustion. Electricity comes into a house as a main's supply. However, it is worth recording here several alternative sources that could come into more extended use, particularly in the more remote country districts.

Wind Generators

It is reported that small domestic wind-driven generators likely to produce 2–3Kw are likely to be marketed shortly in the USA (see illustration).

Water Generators

Any householder with a small stream running through their property could install one of the domestic-size electricity turbines now available. The energy output is likely to be more constant than that of wind generators rising to about 4Kw.

Photoic Cells

These cells are readily available in the USA and will shortly be sold in the UK. They generate direct current electricity when exposed to sunlight or heat. At present the output is restricted to about 25 volts, but this will increase as larger models are evolved.

Thermoelectric Generators

This is a variant of the Thermovolt photoic cell. The Thermacell is a solid state device which will generate an electric current from the heat of cookers and room heaters that would otherwise be wasted. It is expected to generate up to 150 watts. (See Useful Addresses.)

Compost Generators

A German company is marketing a unit for producing small outputs of electricity from the heat generated by the decomposition of farmyard and domestic waste. The supply is steady as the exhausted waste is continually replaced with fresh organic material (dung, vegetable waste, household refuse, etc).

Gas

Gas fuel piped into the house by British Gas, a national industry, is clean, convenient, and supplied under terms that virtually preclude any DIY installation.

Bottled Gas

The Calor Gas company supplies (under a variety of trade names across the country) two types of gas in liquid form under pressure in metal containers. Both are categorised as methane gases. Butane is produced by the dry distillation of organic substances. Propane is dissolved out from crude petroleum oil. The two gases are indistinguishable in ordinary performance, both producing a short, hard flame.

Both gases are marketed throughout the rural districts of the UK, wherever piped gas is not available, and form an adequate, although expensive, alternative. Propane, however, has a lower freezing temperature and is, therefore, better suited to colder regions than Butane.

When bottled gas is to be used to fuel a central heating system, it is best to install a large pressure tank (see photograph) somewhere close to the house, but not adjacent to it. This container can be replenished regularly

Photo 19 Typical Calor bottled gas cylinders showing the 'switch-over' valve from an empty cylinder to a full one

Photo 20 Country homes can be supplied with a liquid gas (Calor Gas) cylinder, the equivalent of an oil tank, and filled at intervals by mobile tankers

by tanker vehicles. The agreement by which the company contracts for this supply removes (properly) the possibility of non-professional work.

Should the gas be required only for cooking, smaller, portable cylinders are available. These should not be stored inside the house because of the slight risk of explosion should there be a gas leak.

Apart from the final connection to the domestic cooker, the work of running the supply pipe into the house through the outer wall can be undertaken by an experienced DIY enthusiast.

Small gas cylinders are included within the casing of portable domestic gas heaters. Care should be taken that these are only used in properly ventilated rooms as an evening's use can result in the walls streaming with condensation.

There are no building regulation requirements concerning the use of bottled gas cylinders in the home. There is, however, a Code of Practice that all permanent installations should place the gas cylinder outside the house. In the rare event of a cylinder valve leak, gas escaping into the house could asphixiate the residents, or cause serious explosions.

Oil

In the Fifties and Sixties fuel oil heralded the era of central heating. Previously, each individual room in the average UK home was heated independently. Oil-fired central heating made it more convenient to heat the home as a single unit (although other types of radiator heating had existed before).

Oil's two main features were its relative cheapness and its convenience. Controlled by thermostats, oil-fired boilers switched them-

Photo 21 Baxi floor-standing gas boiler

Photo 22 Trianco wall-mounted gas boiler

Photo 23 The Trianco Homeflame gas cylinder heater for hearth fixing only

Photo 24 A modern paraffin heater from Godin Stoves of France

selves on and off (or raised and lowered the rate of burn) to sustain any pre-selected temperature.

The international crises of the early seventies eroded oil's popularity and supremacy. Supplies were interrupted and it became more expensive than the more traditional fuels. It remains relatively costly today.

Houses that are still heated by oil are vulnerable to replacement by alternatives. Mains (ie, piped) gas-fired central heating is cheaper and at least as convenient. Pressure-tank supplies of methane are more expensive than piped gas and less convenient in that a storage tank must be installed.

Electric storage heaters with their cheap-rate overnight tariffs are a strong competitor in the central-heating market and the first automatic coal-fired boiler has just come onto the market.

Paraffin

For those who prefer to sit beside a fire they can see, even if only through a glass window, fuel oil never supplied an answer, but paraffin (kerosene) continues to fuel a dwindling range of portable heaters that satisfy this need. Regular use inevitably results in the characteristic paraffin smell. Although heat outputs are relatively low, paraffin remains one of the least expensive fuels.

4 Stoves, Fires and Boilers

The Box Stove

The simplest type of solid-fuel burning, free-standing room heater is the box stove. As its name implies, at the simplest level it consists of a metal box – made either of cast-iron panels or sheets of welded steel – with or without legs. From a performance viewpoint there is nothing to choose between these two constructions. What is of greater importance is the design of the stove itself, the quality of manufacture and the weight of metal used.

Internally, the stove may have a baffle to guide the fire-gas toward the chimney flue and to swirl the gas around the fire-chamber so that more of its heat is picked up by the metal walls and radiated into the living-room.

Most box stoves have a fire-bed or basket allowing them to burn both wood and solid fuel. More elaborate models may have a glass panel in the front door (as in the French Godin Art Deco), or a hot-plate on the top surface for simple cooking (as in the Danish Morsø Models 1440, 1540 and 1510).

Being free-standing, the box stove can stand in the house wherever your heat flow chart suggests (see pp 17–22). This placing must, however, conform to building regulations requirements (see p 92).

The essential design element of the box stove is that it is air-tight. Consequently, the flow of air into its fire can be regulated exactly. A bottom vent, either in the form of a rotating plate or disc, or as a sliding trap, provides the first line of control. A butterfly valve at the base of the flue regulates the rise of hot fire-gas into the chimney

While stoves of this design have never achieved popularity in Britain, they have remained firm favourites in Europe where they are marketed as cheap, reliable and long-lasting heaters.

In Britain, the cylinder stove – as in the Broomside Arctic and Epping stoves – fulfils much the same role as the box stove, although of a different shape. Servicemen

Photo 25 Morsø 1410 Box stove from Denmark

45

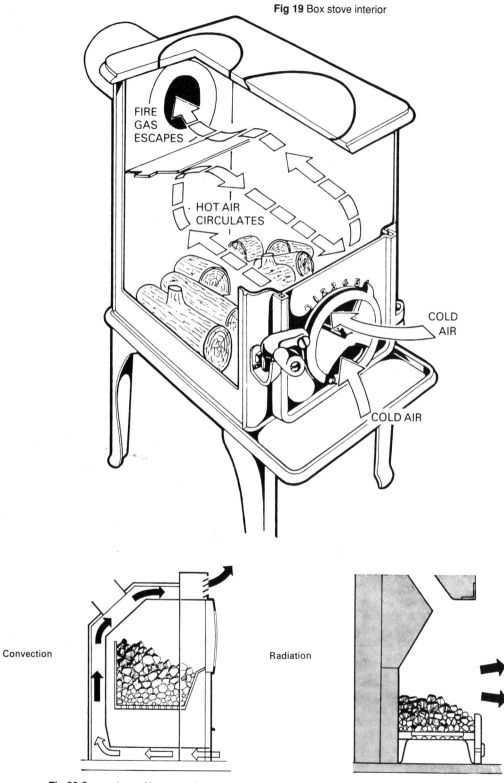

Fig 19 Box stove interior

FIRE
GAS
ESCAPES

HOT AIR
CIRCULATES

COLD
AIR

COLD AIR

Convection

Radiation

Fig 20 Comparison of heat transfer between the Inset stove (*left*) and the open hearth (*right*)

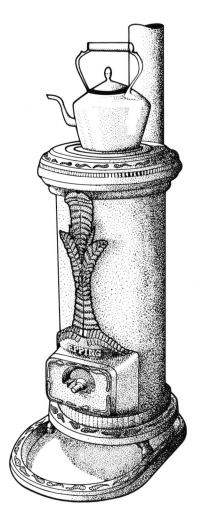

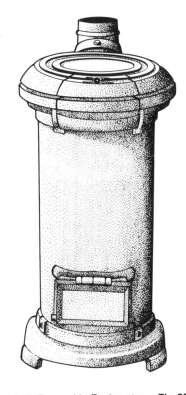

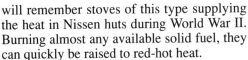

will remember stoves of this type supplying the heat in Nissen huts during World War II. Burning almost any available solid fuel, they can quickly be raised to red-hot heat.

Box stoves can usually be fitted with simple water boilers with enough capacity to supply perhaps one or two radiators, or a minimal hot water supply. As inexpensive, basic heaters, they remain an excellent choice.

The Glass-fronted Stove

Produced in response to the British householder's demand to see the flames the glass-fronted stove is supplied in such a variety of styles and sizes that only a general description is possible here.

Fig 21 (*left*) Broomside Epping stove; **Fig 22** (*right*) Broomside Arctic stove

Most manufacturers supply both multi-fuel and solid fuel versions. Very few of these multi-fuel designs have developed a wholly satisfactory dual-purpose grate, ie one that can change from burning wood to solid fuel. Rotating and reciprocating fire-bars are available. All have a tendency to jam, distort under heat, or fail to modify the air flow into the fire (above the ash-bed for wood, from below for solid fuel).

One stove that solves most of these problems is the patented Aarrow design in which alternate fire-bars interact forwards and backwards differentially, with a variable clearance between. The Charnwood stove from the Isle of Wight (see Useful Addresses) has a similar

47

Photo 26 The Dovre Hostess – multi-cooker and roomheater

Photo 27 Parkray GL Roomheater for solid fuel

Photo 28 Jetmaster centrally-placed open fire multi-fuel stove

Photo 29 Aarrow Stratford stove from Dorset (designed for the American market)

Photo 30 The Dovre 2000 fan-assisted multi-fuel
stove from Holland

Photo 31 The Franco-Belge 'Normandie' stove from France

Photo 32 The Charnwood stove from the Isle of Wight

Photo 33 The Nestor-Martin Retro stove from Belgium

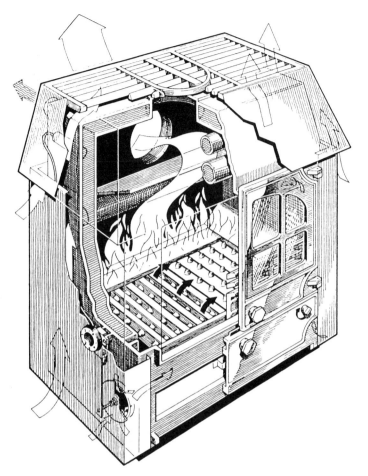

Fig 23 Cutaway diagram illustrating heat distribution of a Charnwood convector stove

design of adjustable fire bars that is also effective (see illustration above).

Glass-fronted stoves are worked in much the same way as box stoves (see p 45).The tendency for tar in wood-burning models to precipitate on the inner surface of the glass can be cured by working the stove hard (ie hot) for 15–20 minutes each day. This will liquefy and burn away the tar. Any residue can be dissolved, when the glass is cool, with household paraffin.

The main functional advantage of the free-standing, glass-fronted stove is that it supplies both direct heat from the fire and radiant heat from all its surfaces (sides, top, back and front) into the living space. A disadvantage of this arrangement is that children and the elderly may inadvertently touch the hot stove and burn themselves.

In some designs an outer casing of sheet metal covers the inner fire-box. This outer casing never becomes more than warm and so prevents injury. The air in the gap between the two surfaces is warmed and rises into the room by convection.

The Insert Stove

Stoves of this kind are a cross between the open fire and the free-standing heater. Indeed, with such a variety of models available, it is often difficult to decide which categorisation applies.

There are open fires set right back in the fire-chamber with elaborate draughting arrangements and there are air-tight stoves that do not quite connect with the structure of the hearth (see photographs). The term hole-in-the-wall heater is often applied to make the precise classification more clear.

Photo 34 Vermont Castings Insert Fireplace from the USA

Photo 36 The Stack Vista high-energy combustion stove from New Zealand

Photo 35 Parkray Coalmaster II Insert stove

In essence, insert stoves are intended to sit back into the space that would otherwise be occupied by a fireplace, thereby renouncing the freedom of placing enjoyed by the free-standing stove. Another disadvantage is that heat from the sides, top and back of the fire-box is fed into the surrounding wall and does not directly warm the air in the living-room. If, as is often the case, the fireplace is on an outer wall, some part of the heat it generates will be lost through the exterior. However, in a smallish room, the insert model can save valuable space.

As inserts have the same high burning efficiency as the free-standing variety, there is generally no difficulty in heating a room, circulating hot water to several radiators and supplying domestic hot water. Depending on the model, it is sometimes possible to remove the insert heater as a complete unit when moving house.

As with free-standing, air-tight stoves, inserts will comfortably burn overnight, especially when using solid fuels.

DIY Stoves by Kedddy

Right on the practical limits of DIY installation is a series of stoves marketed in the UK by Kedddy Ltd. Their inclusion here is justified because they represent the end of a connected chain of stove design philosophy that emanates from Scandinavia, a region that has had a dominant influence on stove design in Britain.

It can be argued that virtually all wood stoves marketed in Britain in the late Seventies were based on existing Norwegian and Danish models that were also being imported here. The cast-iron Norwegian Jøtul No 6 was copied in Britain as a sheet-metal welded unit. Glass-fronted models were based on Danish ideas. The emergence of multi-fuel models to bridge the gap between wood-fuel and coal-fuel supplies in Great Britain has hardly modified the connection.

The development of low BTU gas generators (fed by wood-chips) in Sweden, although having a negligible impact here, has none the less sustained Scandinavian supremacy in domestic heating system design.

The Kedddy models featured here are, perhaps, the most refined examples to date of that heating philosophy. Certainly, for the

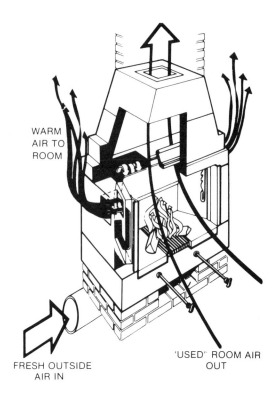

WARM AIR TO ROOM

FRESH OUTSIDE AIR IN

'USED' ROOM AIR OUT

Fig 24 The Kedddy Superfire

readers of this book they pave the way for the introduction of specific Swedish ideas that advance efficient home-heating several stages further forward, and tie the knot between heat generation, distribution and the most effective placing of the stove in the house – themes with which this book began.

As the illustrations show (on p 55) the Kedddy Superfire model comes as a prefabricated kit of parts moulded in lightweight concrete (a few parts may be too heavy for some people to lift easily). It incorporates underfloor air supply, generally from the exterior. As with the fire-chest model described on p 88, a foundation block is cemented to the top of the constructional hearth once the air channel into the back of the stove is connected. Thereafter, simple step-by-step construction completes the assembly (see illustration).

The flue lintel, with air controls, is fitted on top of the fire-chest which is lined with firebricks and fitted with a grate. The top of the stove is then ready to receive the first section of chimney, the erection of which is described fully on p 55.

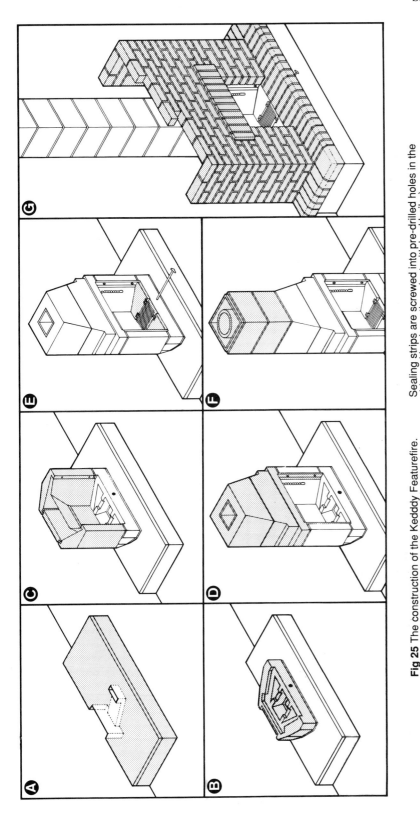

Fig 25 The construction of the Kedddy Featurefire.
A. Construct underhearth with air supply
B. Having already provided the underhearth air supply and adequate foundations, the air damper securing strap (provided for transit only) is removed and the base section is bedded onto mortar
C. The steel support angle is placed above the air damper on the base section. The back section is bedded on followed by the side sections which retain the back. The fireback is then inserted loose
D. The flue lintel (complete with damper and control) and flue gather units are bedded on the side and back.

Sealing strips are screwed into pre-drilled holes in the side and back sections (not with backboiler)
E. The firebricks and grate are fitted onto the base section. The underhearth air control handle and extension rod are fitted and their operation tested
F. The first sections of the appropriate chimney system are fitted
G. The required framing and facing are built-up around the Featurefire to ceiling level. The extension rod to the air control should be cut to the required length and the handle fitted. The Featurefire should be left for one week before use

55

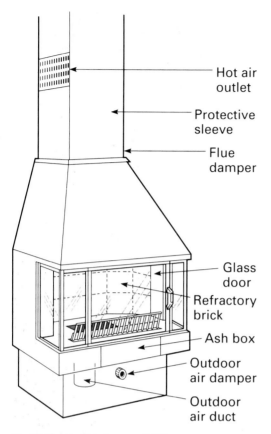

Hot air outlet

Protective sleeve

Flue damper

Glass door

Refractory brick

Ash box

Outdoor air damper

Outdoor air duct

Fig 26 The Kedddy Contura C-350

The Contura model, which is manufactured in Sweden, is a metal-box unit housed in concrete and is intended to be free-standing, rather than wall-mounted. This stove delivers direct radiant heat from the fire, radiated heat from the stove sides, the hood and chimney-breast, convected hot air, and can include hot-water boilers.

The Closed Stove

Installing a closed stove is no more difficult than fitting an open fire. If the house in question was built without either a chimney or hearth, then these must be prepared in advance to receive the stove unit (see pp 83, and 85–8). A register plate must be fitted to seal the base of the existing chimney, if there was one (see illustration p 166). This will leave a connection into the flue-pipe ready to receive the outlet pipe from the stove (either top- or rear-mounted.

When the stove is delivered, a number of strong people will be needed to lift it into place. (Depending on the size, the weight of a stove case, either made of cast iron or welded steel, can be as much as 275–315kg (600–700lb). A sack truck will be adequate to carry it through the house from the delivery van, although some hoisting will be necessary if there are steps along the route.

When the stove is placed in position on a constructional hearth (see pp 85–8), check that there are the proper clearances between the stove case and any surrounding burnable surfaces and materials (see pp 85–8).

In addition to the metal-band fixings usually provided by the stove-maker, it is important to complete the air seal between the stove flue and the register-plate flue connection with a liberal layer of fire-clay. Make sure this is completely dry before firing the stove.

The manufacturers will supply detailed instructions with the stove, describing firing procedure. At first there will probably be a strong, pungent odour coming from the stove case. This is the paint cover 'curing' and will occur only on the first few firings.

Multi-fuel Stoves

A number of stoves are marketed as multi-fuel models, with some automatic conversion from wood to coal burning, and vice-versa. The concept is that wood burns best on a solid base, with air coming in across its top surface, while coal, which requires about double the air supply of wood, burns best with air rising up through it from below. These conversion grates, therefore, by some mechanical means, allow slots or other apertures to be open for coal and closed for wood burning. By pulling a lever, the grate will open or close, rotate, slide back and forth or reveal openable 'venetian blinds'.

In general, these systems do not work in the manner described in their brochures. To some degree, the conversion from coal to wood is more successful. What is commonly overlooked by the designer of these arrangements is that wood-ash, under heat, bakes to a hard, self-supporting crust so that these interchangeable grates thrash about underneath it and leave the wood-ash layer untouched.

Photo 37 Kedddy Contura Stove

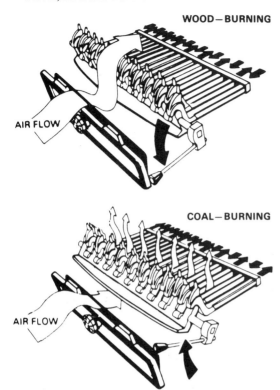

WOOD—BURNING

AIR FLOW

COAL—BURNING

AIR FLOW

Fig 27 The Aarrow dynamic non-jamming multi-fuel grate

Only one model, tested by the author, offers an effective change-over mechanism. This is the Aarrow series of stoves distributed under the names 'Hamlet' and 'Astra'. In these stoves there is no fixed, one-piece fire-grate. Instead, the fire-bed is made of a series of single, independently mounted fire-bars (see illustration). Installed in pairs, the rear end of each bar rests on a ledge across the rear of the fire-chamber, while the front end rests on a cam that extends horizontally across the front of the stove case. When a lever at the side of the case is raised and lowered, these fire-bars move relative to each other. In each pair, as one bar moves forward, its neighbour slides backwards, and vice-versa. In addition, there is implanted in each fire-bar's movement an upward 'kick' so that any ash or clinker is gradually worked down between the bars into the ash-pit below. Larger pieces are worked back to the rear of the chamber where the space between the bars gradually widens until there is a gap large enough for these big pieces to drop through. Because the bars have no physical

restraint in their upward movement, there is no possibility that they will jam. Should there be any obstruction, the bars will ride up over it, working it back towards the rear where it will eventually drop through. The upward kick in the sequence cuts into the lower surface of the wood-ash crust until it breaks down and is worked through the fire-bars into the ash container.

For those who have no need for an immediate conversion from one burning mode to another, the simplest remedy is to purchase any suitable coal stove. Wood burns readily on open fire-bars and a layer of ash builds up quickly enough even on fire-bars for this to be an effective control of the air flow into the fire. Alternatively, the fire-grate can be removed and the wood fuel burned on the solid floor of the fire-chamber. It may be necessary to remove the ash-tray to do this conveniently.

The Cooker/Stove

There is one particular type of house heater that both limits and extends the options. This is the cooker/stove.

From the earliest times household fires have been used to supply both the heat for cooking and for warming the house, or some part of it. In Victorian times, both in the UK, Europe and North America, large elaborate cast-iron stoves were built for this purpose. The Aga cooker has become a classic of its kind, closely followed by the Rayburn. Modernised versions of both are currently marketed. In Europe, almost every country has one or more modern cooker/stoves in production (see pp 61–2).

Two points must be noted here. First, there is, to a degree, a strong separation between the manufacturing philosophies of the UK and Europe. In Britain, such a stove, being for most household budgets relatively expensive, tends to be thought of as a once-in-a-lifetime purchase, and is constructed accordingly. There is at least one firm that specialises in converting old British stoves to more modern fuel use (see Useful Addresses, Country Cookers Ltd). In Europe, the cooker/stove has become a 'consumer durable' with a comparable working life. Householders are inclined to repurchase every few years to secure the latest model, as they do with cars.

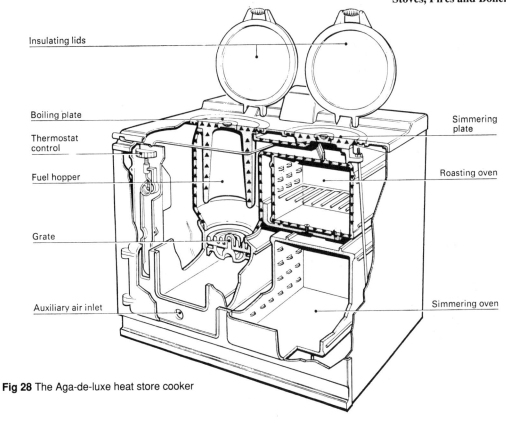

Insulating lids

Boiling plate

Thermostat control

Fuel hopper

Grate

Auxiliary air inlet

Simmering plate

Roasting oven

Simmering oven

Fig 28 The Aga-de-luxe heat store cooker

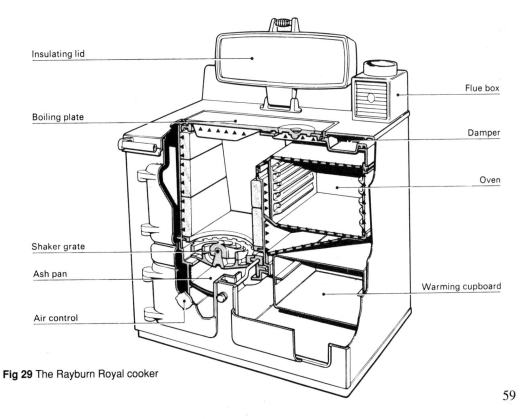

Insulating lid

Boiling plate

Shaker grate

Ash pan

Air control

Flue box

Damper

Oven

Warming cupboard

Fig 29 The Rayburn Royal cooker

59

Photo 38 The Bosky Cooker – a combined Italian/British production

Photo 39 The Rayburn Cooker

60

Photo 40 The Tirolia Casanove Lux
multi-fuel cooker from Austria

Photo 41 The Franco-Belge
Première cooker from France

61

Photo 42 The French Chatelaine Cooker made by Godin

Secondly, careful planning needs to be applied to everyday cooker/stove use because, in practice, the gentler heating mode for household heating does not supply the fiercer heat required for cooking. Conversely, strong cooking heat is more than is needed for house-heating. When worked with wood fuel exclusively, cookers often have tarring problems in the smoke chambers that surround the ovens, requiring regular cleaning to keep them clear. None the less, these heaters can be valuable additions to a household if properly mastered.

The cooker/stove is restricted to placement in the kitchen, preferably against an inner wall. Factors that modify the best locations are the type of house layout (ie open plan or individual rooms), and the type of central heating chosen (ie hot air or hot water).

The Open Fire

By far the most popular, and cheapest, solid fuel heater in Britain is the open-fire grate. In a chamber below a chimney, standing on a non-combustible hearth, the grate consists of fire-bars with supporting legs, and retaining bars across the front to hold in the fuel. If you wish to burn wood, the grate can be removed by lifting it out. Indeed, it is not even essential to do that, as wood will burn quite satisfactorily on the fire-bars.

As the grate is fully exposed to the atmosphere with no restraints, it is not possible to regulate the air flow significantly. For this reason, open fires have only about a third of

Photo 43 The Parietale 005

Photo 44 The Ligne Actuelle 937

Photo 45 The Ligne Actuelle 931

Photo 46 The Ligne Actuelle 936

Photo 47 Lion basket dog grate

Photo 48 Maxiwarm Firebrick Heat Exchanger

Photo 49 Tortoise Convector Box-in-a-box stove

the burning efficiency of the equivalent closed stoves as most of the heat generated is wasted up the chimney. Most British families, however, seem to be willing to make this sacrifice to enjoy the pleasure of sitting beside an open fire.

The loss of heat can be mitigated in two main ways. By restricting the flow of fire-gas up the chimney flue, the rate of burn can be slowed to some degree. This retains more heat for distribution inside the living space. In addition, by mounting a box-within-a-box with the fire burning inside the inner box (see photograph), air in the gap between the boxes is heated. It rises and escapes into the living-room (being sealed off from the chimney) where it circulates as warm convected air. The introduction of both these arrangements raises the efficiency of the open fire to about half that of the closed stove.

Photo 50 A typical open fire grate

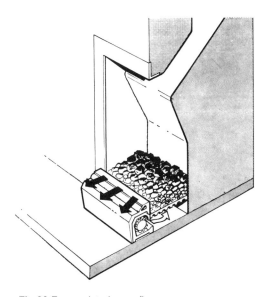

Fig 30 Fan-assisted open fire

As a further refinement, it is possible to feed air into the fire from the space beneath the floor or hearth. This reduces or eliminates draughts into the room and so helps to keep the living space warm.

Basic open fire grates are available from stove dealers and ironmongers at a very modest cost. (Some fuel manufacturers, such as Coalite, market these as special promotions). A typical model would be 406mm (16in) wide and would come supplied with an overnight burning plate (see photograph). The grate would be a single piece of cast iron and would consist of a framework of fire bars with supporting feet. There would be a standard size to fit into the standard fireplace recess (16in) and probably non-standard sizes for other applications.

The space below the fire-bars is used to catch the ash and clinker from the fire. Sometimes an ash-pan is available which must be cleared regularly to prevent the ash from blocking the flow of air into the fire. If there is no ash-pan, a retaining lip along the front edge of the fireplace recess is a useful idea. Clearance is with a small hand-shovel.

The Underfloor Draught Fire

One of the more efficient forms of open fire is that which takes most of its air from the space under the flooring or from the exterior. Two typical models are featured here, illustrative of the general principles and forms of construction.

As can be seen from the two illustrations, air is piped or ducted from the underfloor space (or the exterior of the house) to a chamber below the fire. A butterfly valve controls the rate of entry into the fire, allowing the fire to burn either hot or at a slumber rate.

A point needs to be made here about chimney smoke. There are two main reasons why a chimney releases smoke into the living-room. Either the chimney flue has insufficient capacity to carry the volume of smoke, or there is inadequate ventilation of fresh air into the room where the fire is burning. This is of prime importance with underfloor draughted fires. If ventilators or airbricks are blocked, smoke cannot escape up the chimney at a greater rate than fresh air is available to flow in to replace it. If it could, a vacuum would be formed in the living-room, which is an impossibility. Alternatively, the fire may burn too rapidly, and thereby wastefully, if too much fresh air is allowed to enter the living-room. This means that doors and windows must not be opened at a greater aperture than necessary to keep the fire burning at a controlled rate.

Ash removal from underfloor draught fires is from a chamber below floor level. Usually it is only necessary to clear the ash every four to seven days. Often, for convenience, it is possible to remove ash from outside the house.

A fire-bar allows a large load of fuel to be placed on the fire, making overnight burning for periods of up to eight hours or more quite practicable.

It should be noted that processed petroleum-based fuels should not be used on stoves of this type, which are generally intended to be worked with solid fuel and possible wood.

Back-boilers or wrap-around boilers are usually available and these provide a useful additional source of heat in the form of hot water.

The Box-in-a-box Fire

There are basically two ways of improving the performance of an open fire. They are both eighteenth century in concept, although manufacturers claim them as modern.

The first is the simplest. As the title suggests, it consists of two fire-chambers, one mounted inside the other. At the base of this double chamber there is an air entry into the gap between the two and another air exit at the top of the stove, leading from the air gap. The fire is worked exactly as if it were a plain open fire, but as the fire heats up, it warms the air in the gap between the two chambers. This air rises by convection and escapes into the living space through the gap at the top. It is replaced by fresh air which is pulled in through the bottom air opening so that, in addition to the direct radiant heat coming from the fire, there is also a continuous flow of warm air feeding into the living-room. This improves the fire's performance by 5–10 per cent. The total heat output remains well below that achieved by the best closed stoves. However, it is a welcome improvement on the open fire and is a sensible compromise.

The second way to improve the performance of stoves of this type is to fit a simple throat control at the base of the chimney flue. Opening or closing this with a lever allows more or less fire-gas to escape to the exterior. This increases or decreases the flow of fresh air into the fire and, thereby, regulates the burning rate. This is a rather primitive and uncertain form of control.

Installation of a box-in-a-box fire is virtually identical with that for a plain 'metal-box' open fire. It requires a constructional hearth to stand on and a flue entry into the base of the chimney.

The Decorative Fireplace

The Basic fireplace as described on p 92 and pp 118–19 can be given a façade decoration. As there are hundreds of designs and styles available, only a general sample can be given here.

In their simplest form, decorative effects do nothing to amplify the performance of the fire. It remains an open fire with all the imperfections that the term implies. Many

Photo 51 Underfloor Draught Fireplace

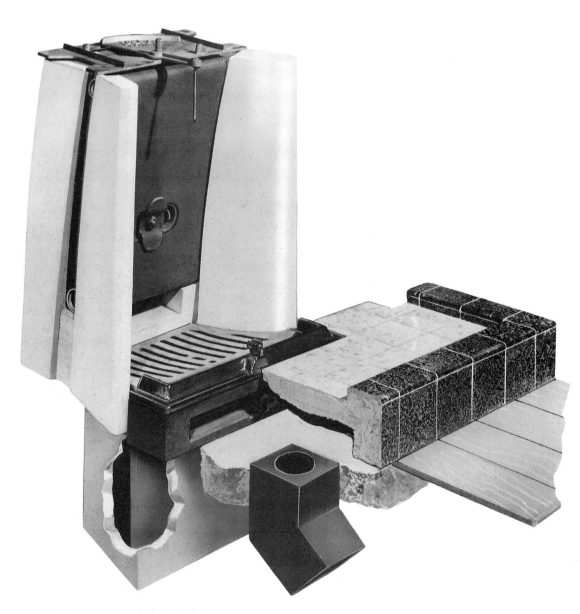

Photo 52 Underfloor/Draught Fireplace

Photo 53 Dovre Convection Box

Photo 54 Handcrafted fireplace surrounds by Hallidays of Dorchester-on-Thames

householders install a decorative open fire not primarily as a source of house heat, which is often supplied by a background central heating system, but for the comfort and pleasure of being able to sit beside a blazing fire.

Decorative fireplaces are usually purchased in kit form, for DIY or professional installation. Some are extremely elaborate and expensive. One company at Dorchester-on-Thames creates hand-carved wooden reproductions of classic Georgian designs. Prices are inevitably in four figures. Middle-of-the-range designs (ie £400–£600) include models made of continental smooth brick, polished marble, natural stone, sand-faced briquettes, African quartzite, stainless steel and glazed ceramic tiles with sparkguards of aluminium, stainless steel or brass. Mantels

are formed from mahogany, waxed pine, fibreglass and tessellated (ie decorated) tiles.

Minor adjustments in size to accommodate the dimensions of individual fireplaces can usually be accomplished without difficulty. Natural full-size displays are to be found in many showrooms around the country. Fireplaces of this kind are delivered as packed kits, ready for simple assembly, with instructions enclosed. No competent DIY enthusiast should have any difficulty in mounting a decorative façade in place.

Provided the original fireplace recess complies with building regulations, there are no additional stipulations to be observed.

Combination Features

Such is the strength of the commercial competition in the domestic heater market that, with a proliferation of ideas, some over-lapping of concepts is inevitable.

In the previous two sections, fireplaces with decorative features and convection heaters built on the box-in-a-box principle have been described. The offerings of other makers bridge the gap between these two design ideas. In doing so, they offer further solutions to the specific heating problems of individual families. In a work of this size, it is impossible to describe every model available. Two, therefore, must stand as being typical of many others on offer.

The Tortoise Conqueror fire-box incorporates a back-boiler, combustion air control, adjustable multi-fuel grate, chimney-flue throat control, convected warm air supply, etc. It also has a deep flange surrounding the front frame that allows it to be fitted into a range of fireplace recess openings. A variety of decorative trims also fit onto this flange.

The heater has an under-bar igniter, a type of built-in gas poker that simplifies fire-lighting.

The same company makes the Cinderella, a simple fireplace cleaning unit. One pipe attaches to the domestic vacuum cleaner while the other is used to suck up ash and clinker from the fire-bed, to be stored in a cylindrical container.

Another bridging design is the 'Sunfire' from Kedddy. This, too, can be seen as the precursor of more elaborate heating units. As a convector, inset or insert fire, with double glass-panelled front doors, it occupies a half-way position between the fixed open fire and the flexible air-tight stove.

Multi-fuel Heating

Installing a central heating system is an expensive investment and should only be justified by the higher standard of domestic comfort and the long-term financial saving it offers over other forms of less efficient heating.

There are many types of multi-fuel heating, notably European units such as the Oranier Cosmos from Germany that, in the one appliance, allows the heating to be switched from gas to solid fuel, to oil, at will. The vindication for such an installation is that, for one reason or another, each particular

Fig 31 The Tortoise Conqueror fire-box

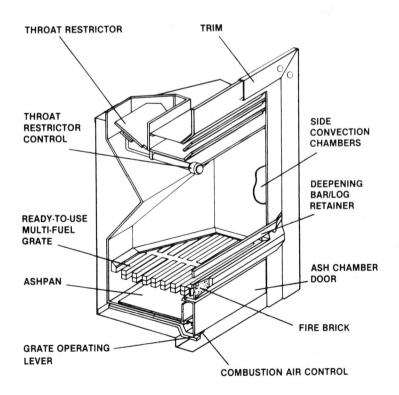

THROAT RESTRICTOR

TRIM

THROAT RESTRICTOR CONTROL

SIDE CONVECTION CHAMBERS

DEEPENING BAR/LOG RETAINER

READY-TO-USE MULTI-FUEL GRATE

ASHPAN

ASH CHAMBER DOOR

FIRE BRICK

GRATE OPERATING LEVER

COMBUSTION AIR CONTROL

Photo 55 Cinderella fireplace vacuum cleaner

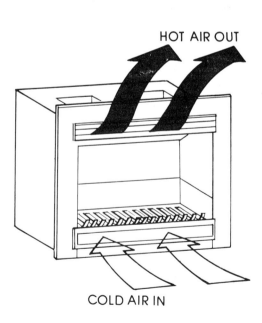

HOT AIR OUT

COLD AIR IN

Fig 32 Kedddy Sunfire convector heater

Photo 56 Oranier Cosmos gas and automatic solid fuel stove from Germany

fuel is the most convenient or the least costly at any specific time of day (ie overnight off-peak electricity, or the fast pick-up and instant heat of gas heating).

This philosophy can be advanced a stage further. Such heating installations require that the heat produced be utilised immediately. This focuses attention on the means of heat distribution in the house, either by hot air or hot water. It may not always be convenient, however, to use the heat so produced at once. A newer concept is now evolving based on an expanding technology of heat storage. This suggests that heat generators of whatever type (ie traditional combustion heaters; wind, wave and solar generators; air, water and soil heat exchangers, liquid-gas burners, biomass digesters, etc) produce heat in their own best way and time, and that heat be stored for use as and when the household needs it. The heat storage units would be in the form of under-ground insulated water (or some other liquid) tanks. Their capacity would be anything from 1,364 to 13,640 litres (300 to 3,000 gal).

These concepts and ideas have yet to be put into practice, although that may not be far distant. For the present, a link between these various heat sources can be found in the concept of 'integrated heat' which has been developed in Sweden by Lars Tjernstrom.

Integrated Heat Appliances

A Swedish Air Force engineer who has turned his mind to the problems of fuel use and heat energy distribution, Lars Tjernstrom has created a range of appliances marketed under the name 'Loggger'. They are manu-factured in a small factory several hundred miles to the north of Stockholm.

Wherever they are placed in the home (ie

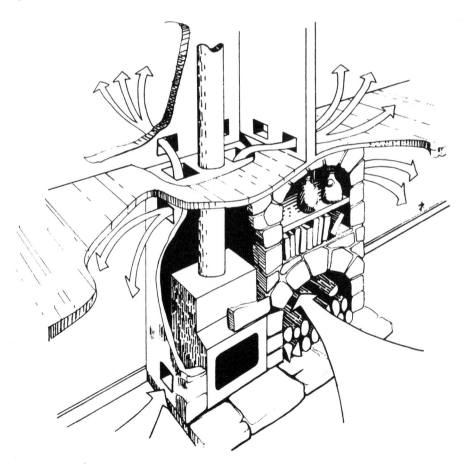

Fig 33 Loggger Featurefire. This diagram shows how it can be used to heat other rooms in the house

Photo 57 The Logggger stove

even against a wall or in a corner) these heaters remain essentially free-standing units, ie their placement in the house needs only to be governed by the demands of best performance.

As with all enthusiasts, Tjernstrom's ideas, if carried to their ultimate expression, would result in bulky and expensive installations. However, when scaled down to the economics and space availability of the medium-sized UK home (ie 3–5 bedrooms), they do offer the prospect of attractive and effective heating.

As the photograph shows, the simplest Logggger stove is placed at the centre of the house with radiant and convected heat emanating from it to warm all the living areas. A more elaborate version adds the facility to duct hot air to those regions of the home beyond the reach of direct convection and radiation and in addition to create focuses of heat at chosen locations.

The most complex model adds hot-water distribution without increasing the size of the stove unit or increasing fuel consumption significantly. Largely, the heat produced is more fully and efficiently utilised.

These three design concepts of integrated

Photo 58 The Logggger Insert stove

heating are marketed in different model forms, of which the following are typical:

1 A living-room fire with underfloor draughting
2 An inglenook heater
3 A central heating unit (hot water and air)
4 A DIY kit complete with chimney flue
5 A total (one source) house-heating system

Boilers

Most room heaters, ie box, glass-fronted and insert stoves, can be fitted with boilers. These usefully extract additional heat from the fire without any increase in the cost of fuel. In other words, boilers absorb heat that would otherwise be wasted up the chimney.

There are two types of boiler: back- and wrap-around. Both can be 'bolt-on' additions or integral to the stove's structure. These same descriptions apply equally to cast-iron stoves or those made of welded sheet steel.

Boilers are generally made of welded steel (although cast-iron types are still occasionally found). More expensive versions are made of copper (even, rarely, of brass). In

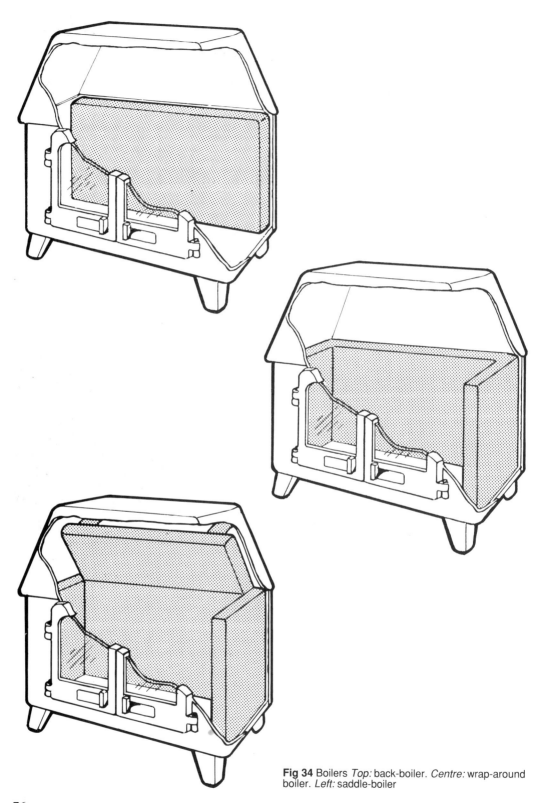

Fig 34 Boilers *Top:* back-boiler. *Centre:* wrap-around boiler. *Left:* saddle-boiler

Photo 59 Aga-Rayburn Rembrandt with high out-put back-boiler

Photo 60 *left* The Dunsley/Baxi high output back boiler with underfloor draught open fire

Photo 61 *right* The Gaelwood Conserva from Scandinavia – a solid-fuel brick central heating unit

Photo 62 The CTC S-70 boiler for burning wood or coal

Photo 65 Dunsley Condor boiler unit of modern style

Photo 63 A high output boiler from Country Cookers that converts standard Rayburn cookers to central heating units

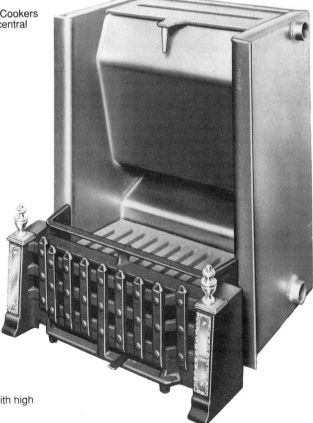

Photo 64 The Ouzledale Regal fire place with high output boiler

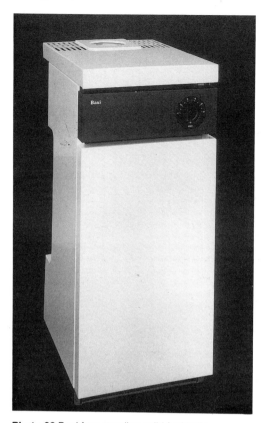

Photo 66 Baxi free-standing solid fuel boiler

When small electric fans are added to improve the fire's performance by blowing fresh air through it, this, if anything, makes the back-boiler proportionately less efficient. Additional electrical energy is being used to make the fire work. This must be deducted from the fire's total heat energy output before the fire's positive heat energy total can be determined. Meanwhile, the fan tends to make the fire-gas rise more rapidly so that, not only is an outside source of energy being used up, but the fire-gas is having even less contact with the back-boiler.

An improvement on the back-boiler is the wrap-around which is generally incorporated in closed stoves although open fires can be equipped in this way. The stove wall is double-skinned and the narrow gap between the two metal skins (usually less than 25mm (1in) thick) is filled with water. Because it surrounds the fire, its heat pick-up is more rapid and efficiency is much improved. The water absorbs radiant heat from the fire which tends to slow down the speed at which the fire-gas rises, leaving it longer in contact with the back wall of the wrap-around boiler. Such boilers greatly augment the heat output of the fire, supplying direct heat, domestic hot water and even a full central heating system.

The most effective design of all is the saddle-boiler, named because of its resemblance to a horse saddle. The wrap-around walls are linked across the top by a hollow baffle that is also water-filled. Again, the rising fire-gas is stablised. There is increased surface contact, and an increased surface area. Because the gas is moving more slowly, there is the greatest pick-up of radiant heat. As a result, it is possible for a medium-sized saddle-boiler fire to heat an entire central heating system of up to ten large radiators in no more than 30–40 minutes from a cold start.

Self-contained, closed, water-heating units burning wood, solid fuel, gas or oil and with no direct heat input to the house are available for installation in kitchens, outhouses, basements and cellars. They supply domestic hot water and central heating unobtrusively. The solid fuel version with hopper fuel feeds have almost the convenience of gas and oil.

It is important to ensure that the stove/boiler unit installed in the house has an

practice, these distinctions have little effect. The cheapest steel models offer an effective performance and a good working life.

In both open and closed fires the most commonly fitted water-heating device is the back-boiler. As the name implies, it is fitted above the fire on the back wall of the fire chamber, below the chimney flue. It is angled forward to capture more heat and act as a baffle. Even a casual examination reveals the woeful inadequacies of this arrangement. Only a proportion of the fire-gas is ever in contact with the surface of the boiler to transfer heat. The remainder is rapidly wasted up the chimney. The fire-gas is, in any case, travelling so swiftly that no part of it is in contact with the back-boiler for more than a fraction of a second. Very little of the fire's radiant heat flows up towards the back-boiler; most is directed forward and out into the living-room. At best, it will supplement the domestic hot-water supply and heat one or two radiators.

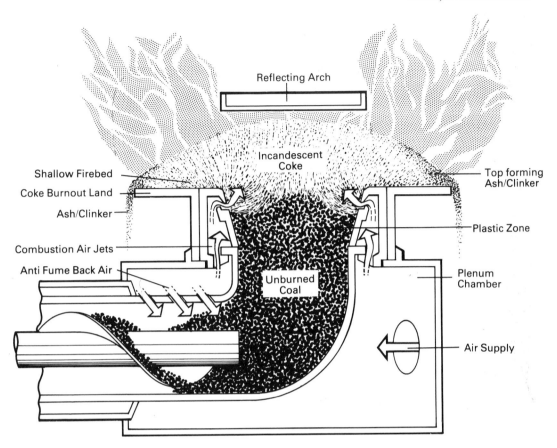

Reflecting Arch

Incandescent
Coke

Shallow Firebed

Coke Burnout Land

Ash/Clinker

Combustion Air Jets

Anti Fume Back Air

Unburned
Coal

Top forming
Ash/Clinker

Plastic Zone

Plenum
Chamber

Air Supply

Fig 35 Self cleaning under feed Stoker Retort

output adequate to the demands to be made of it. Viewed in the showroom, different models will be tagged with their measured heat outputs in kilowatts and British Thermal Units. They are tested by either the National Fireplace Association, or under the auspices of the DSFAAS, The Domestic Solid Fuel Approved Appliance Scheme. DSFAAS tests are conducted by the Coal Research Establishment at Stoke Orchard, near Cheltenham. A separate figure will be given for heat output into the room and heat output into the water jacket (see p 19 for methods of calculating the outputs needed to heat any house).

Gasifiers

Gasifiers come from Scandinavia, particularly Sweden, and are a new type of house heater that will use sap-wet wood straight from felling and with no air-drying necessary. An on-site chipper breaks down the branches and twigs to small pieces. These are fed by a screw auger into a small chamber where they are burnt in an oxygen-starved atmosphere. This produces a low BTU (ie a low heat-producing) gas which can be fed through to the domestic boiler and used to fuel the house central heating (see illustration). Again, such units have not found favour in Britain because of their large size and high cost.

The Heat Store

Many modern American and Scandinavian house-heating systems are based on the use of a heat store, usually in the form of a large, insulated, underground water tank of 1,818–4,546 litres (400–1,000gal capacity). Heat is fed into this tank from whatever source is conveniently available. In the daytime it may be solar heat; on sunless days log fires could

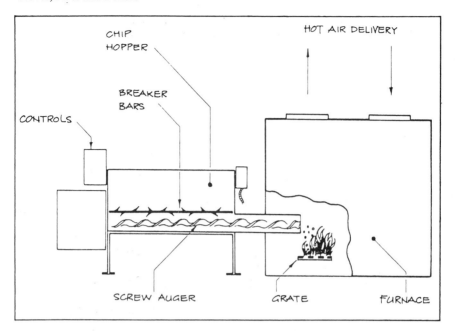

Fig 36 Swedish Gasifer

be lit; overnight cheap electricity may be used. Oil, coal, biomass, wind energy, soil or water heat exchangers and water electricity generators are other possibilities. Heat from this store can be distributed throughout the house by radiators or hot air ducts.

As this system uses many fuels, it is costly to install, but because it always uses the cheapest fuel available at any given time, its pay-back period is not of undue length.

5 Construction and installation regulations

Smoke Control

The Clean Air Act lays down a general framework within which local authorities across the country can introduce legal requirements of their own. For this reason, the precise terms of smoke control enactment varies from place to place within the UK.

Local smoke control legislation determines the districts or areas of smoke control and takes into consideration any local conditions. In general, it is forbidden to light domestic fires with wood sticks and paper in such zones or to burn wood as a fuel (although certain wood-burning stoves have been cleared for such use). Solid coal fuels that are not regarded as smokeless are also prohibited, with the exception of certain appliances that are designed with a smoke-consuming facility to work with non-smokeless fuels. Many modern domestic multi-fuel units now come within this category.

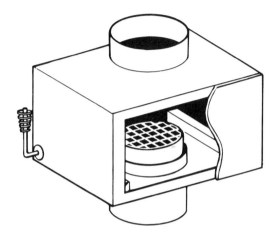

Fig 37 Catalytic converter

Fig 38 Coal-fired room heater with 'smoke-eater' chamber

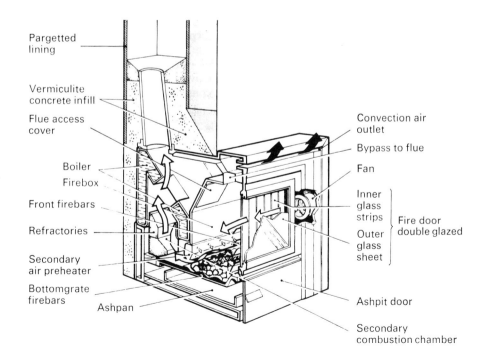

Pargetted lining

Vermiculite concrete infill

Flue access cover

Boiler

Firebox

Front firebars

Refractories

Secondary air preheater

Bottomgrate firebars

Ashpan

Convection air outlet

Bypass to flue

Fan

Inner glass strips

Outer glass sheet

} Fire door double glazed

Ashpit door

Secondary combustion chamber

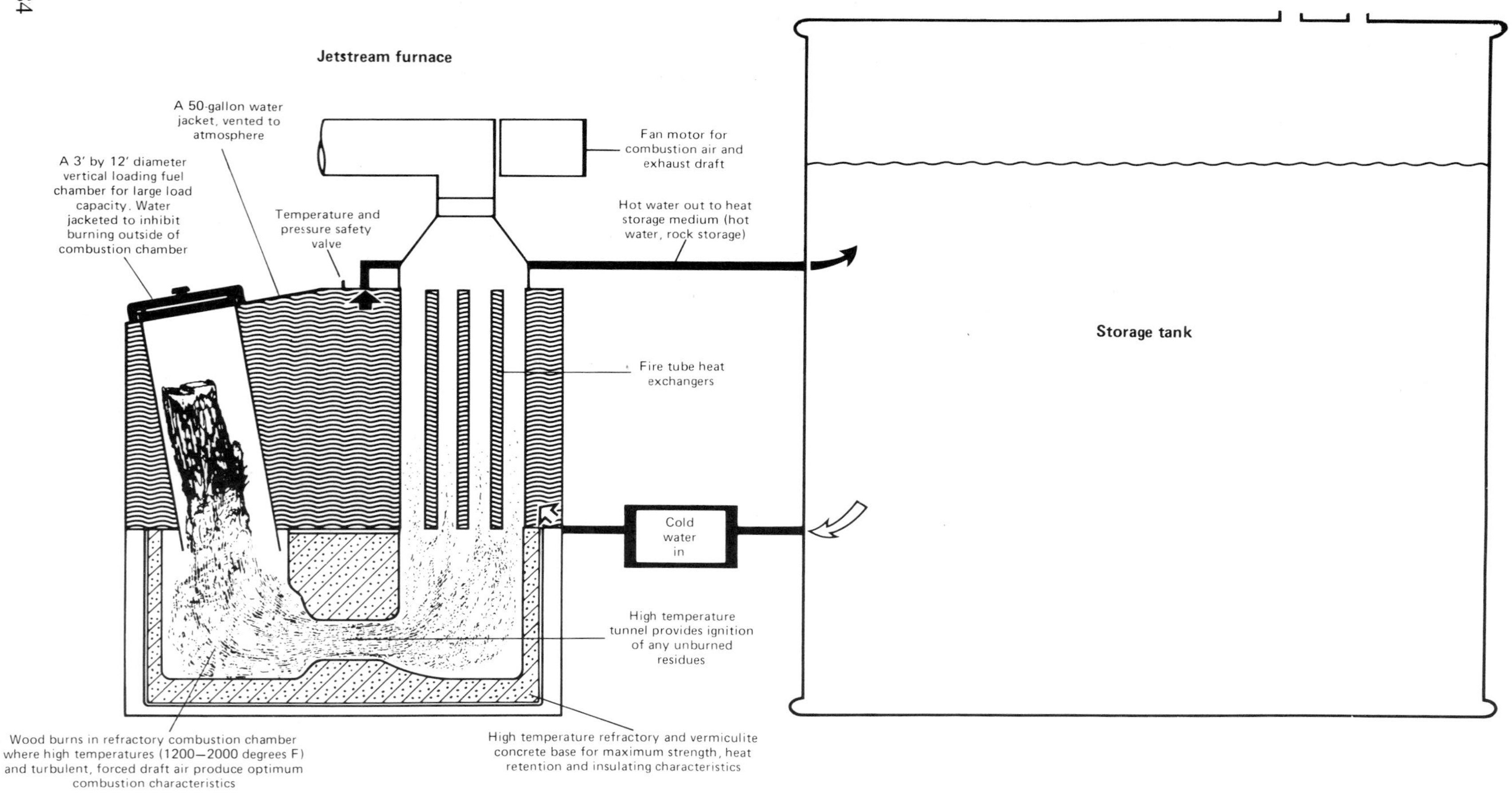

84

Jetstream furnace

A 50-gallon water jacket, vented to atmosphere

Fan motor for combustion air and exhaust draft

Hot water out to heat storage medium (hot water, rock storage)

A 3' by 12' diameter vertical loading fuel chamber for large load capacity. Water jacketed to inhibit burning outside of combustion chamber

Temperature and pressure safety valve

Fire tube heat exchangers

Storage tank

Cold water in

High temperature tunnel provides ignition of any unburned residues

High temperature refractory and vermiculite concrete base for maximum strength, heat retention and insulating characteristics

Wood burns in refractory combustion chamber where high temperatures (1200–2000 degrees F) and turbulent, forced draft air produce optimum combustion characteristics

Fig 39 Jetstream furnace and storage tank

Such stoves rely on one of two basic methods to eliminate smoke. The first is largely of American origin. Introduced a few years ago with much publicity, in practice the unit failed to live up to many of the claims made for it and it was an expensive appliance.

The device was a catalytic converter. The chemical function of a catalyst is to bring about a chemical change in substances with out itself being involved or changed. The American converter was fitted as a filter at the base of the chimney flue. By its presence there, a chemical change was brought about in the hot fire-gas, resulting in the consumption of all those by-products of combustion that were emitted as smoke. These filters proved, in use, not to be completely effective, and after a few months of continuous use had to be replaced at a relatively high cost.

In some American designs – notably, the Jetstream, designed by Dr Richard Hill of the University of Maine in Portland – smoke control is achieved by working the fire at extremely high temperatures, something in excess of 1,090°C (2,000°F) (this is attained by using electrically driven forced draught). Because of this the fire must be contained within a substantial fire-proof concrete chamber. As a result, the unit is weighty, bulky and expensive and has not found favour in European and UK markets. None the less, its cleanliness and overall efficiency cannot be denied.

Other smoke-consuming methods have now been devised, substantially in Britain by the Coal Research Establishment (the research and development arm of the National Coal Board). These allow low-grade household coal – specifically bituminous singles – to be burned in Smoke Control Zones.

The method uses the technique of down-draught firing. Ordinarily, air for combustion rises up through the fire, but certain types of stove have been developed in which combustion air is pulled down into the fire from above. Benefits include more complete combustion of the fuel and less waste of heat in that air remains for longer in contact with the fire and rises less rapidly up the flue.

A smokeless stove currently marketed under the name 'The Worcester', is a free-standing, glass-fronted, closed stove. Its installation poses no more problems than does a conventional model (see p 83). A small electric fan (of about the power of a small light-bulb) drives air down through the fire, which thereby burns more efficiently and at a higher temperature than is usual, consuming some of the smoke particles in the process. Behind the fire is a secondary chamber that is heated by the fire's energy. Fire-gas is forced into this by the action of the fan. It ignites for a second time, burning away all remaining smoke particles. The fire-gas that finally escapes to the exterior is virtually invisible, its presence marked only by a heat haze.

The Constructional Hearth

Assuming that your house has no existing chimney or hearth, once you have decided where to position your fireplace (see p 15), the first task is to install a constructional hearth. This is defined as one forming a part of the structure of the building (as contrasted with the superimposed hearth which does not) and usually takes the form of a concrete slab, not less than 125mm (5in) thick. Such slabs can be bought ready made from a local builder's merchant.

If the ground floor of your house (or the room where the hearth is to be installed) is already made of concrete, and provided it is thick enough, it may qualify as a constructional hearth.

If the flooring is of wood, or similar combustible material, then the hearth must be built separate from it. In addition, the hearth must be supported below the floor level.

Depending on the design of the final installation of stove or fireplace plus prefabricated chimney, it may be necessary to provide enough support for the constructional hearth to be able to bear a total weight of 4 tonnes (see pp 17, 85-8, 96).

Consent must be secured from your local authority building inspector before work begins. If the air gaps between the fire or stove and surrounding material are inadequate, you could be ordered to rebuild the work.

Should you manage to complete the installation without the consent of your building inspector and a subsequent house fire occurs, your failure to comply with building regulations standards may invalidate your house insurance policy.

The slab composing the hearth can be placed anywhere that satisfies building regulations requirements – in general these directives relate to the elimination of fire risk in the house and must be strictly adhered to.

There are two possible arrangements:

1 The slab can be laid so that its top surface is level with the surrounding floor.
2 The slab can be laid so that it projects above the level of the surrounding floor.

The hearth must be made of such a dimension that there is a minimum gap of 300mm (12in) between the floor and the front of the stove, if it is an open-fire model, or a closed stove which when opened can be used as an open fire. In any other case, the gap can be reduced to 225mm (9in). Further, there must be a gap of not less than 150mm (6in) between the back and sides of the stove and any surrounding walls or other vertical surfaces. These gaps, however, may be modified by the insertion of heat shields (see p 26)

It must be emphasised that to avoid any possibility that fire may spread from the stove or fire to any surrounding combustible material in the floor or walls by cinders or radiation, the above air gaps must be the minimum distances of separation between the base of the stove and the edges of the hearth.

Ducts and Pits

The building regulations requirements for a constructional hearth are intended to apply to a hearth of solid, continuous construction. However, this is not always the case. For reasons of improved performance (or appearance), it is often arranged that air is fed into the fire from below, either coming from the space below the floor on which the hearth stands, or from outside the house. In either of these cases, the requirements for a constructional hearth need not be taken as prohibiting the inclusion of an air duct, provided that the following provisions are made:

1 The duct must be solely used to supply combustion air for the fire.
2 The duct must carry air only from outside the house, or from the underfloor space.
3 The duct must be air-tight
4 The duct must be made of non-burnable materials.

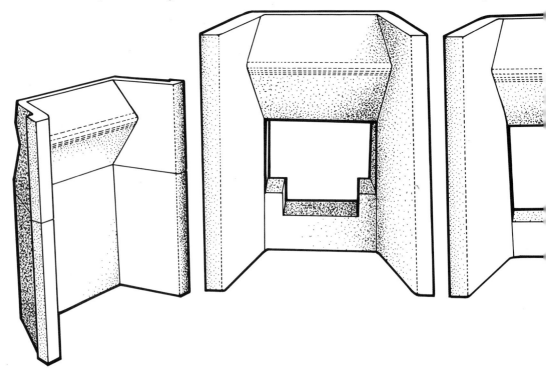

In addition, there are certain relaxations of the regulations to allow for the inclusion of an ash-pit below the hearth. Again, there are certain stipulations:

1 The pit, either to hold ash or an ash container, must have sides and a base made of non-burnable material at least 50mm (2in) thick.

2 There must be no opening in its sides or base, except for the outlet for the duct and an opening to allow ash or the ash container to be removed from outside the building. This opening must be fitted with a close-fitting, non-burnable cover.

3 There must be no burnable material built into the wall below or beside it within 225mm (9in) of its inner surface.

4 There must be a gap of at least 50mm (2in) between the pit's outer surface and any burnable substances placed anywhere other than in the wall below or beside the pit.

These arrangements will allow several days' ash to build up without reducing the fire's performance.

The Superimposed Hearth

A superimposed hearth is one that does not form part of the structure of the building. It must be composed of solid non-combustible material, at least 12.5mm ($\frac{1}{2}$in) thick.

Generally, such a hearth can only be used as a base for a Class II appliance which, in domestic terms, is limited to a gas appliance with an input of heat into the house of less than 60Kw. All other fires of this capacity are graded as Class I appliances and required to stand on a constructional hearth, as previously defined (see pp 85-6).

The Fireplace Recess

In a house that has no hearth or chimney, it is possible to build a fireplace to house either an open or closed fire. In the case of an open fire, one of the central problems to be solved is to create a suitable rising curve up the back wall of the recess to guide the fire-gas into the base of the chimney flue. Various types of

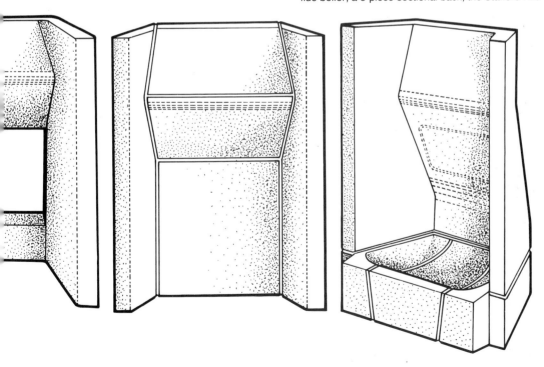

Fig 40 The Fireplace Recess *(from left to right)* Fireclay Milner Back, suitable for use with standard stool and fret; Block Boiler Back, to take any height of block boiler; Arch Boiler Back, to take any height of arch flue boiler; a 5-piece sectional back; the Stafford Fire

moulded fire-brick can be obtained from builders' merchants that help to solve this problem. These are cemented into position with fire-clay.

Certain minimal dimensions are laid down in building regulations for constructing a hearth to form a working foundation for such a fireplace recess. These are what your local building inspector will expect to find when he comes to check your installation.

1 The constructional hearth must extend into the recess right to the back wall and jambs (ie surrounds of the recess).
2 In addition, the hearth must project a minimum of 500mm (20in) in front of the back wall and surrounds.
3 The hearth must also extend forward beyond the fireplace for at least 150mm (6in) in front of each side of the opening.

In the case of a totally free-standing placing (ie well away from the walls of a living area, and possibly even standing right in the centre of a room, open-plan area or large staircase well), where there is no fireplace recess, the dimensions of the constructional hearth must not be less than a square of 840mm (ie a square with sides measuring not less than 33½in).

A fireplace recess and chimney may incorporate a damp-proof course of combustible material as long as it is solidly bedded in cement mortar.

When a fireplace recess is constructed of brick, concrete blocks, burnt clay or concrete cast on site, there must be a jamb or surround on each side that is at least 200mm (8in) thick, together with a solid back wall not less than 200mm (8in) thick. Other materials may be used provided the local authority is satisfied that these are thick enough, have the necessary non-combustible qualities and will adequately prevent ignition spreading to any part of the surrounding house structure. Alternatively, there can be a cavity wall back provided each leaf or section of wall is at least 100mm (4in) thick. These thicknesses are to extend for the full height of the recess.

When the recess is on an external wall and there is no covering of combustible material across the back of the recess, the back may be reduced to a solid wall of at least 100mm (4in) thickness.

Similarly, inside the house, if the wall between two rooms acts as a back to a fireplace recess on both sides (ie back-to-back fireplaces), this wall also needs to be not less than 100mm (4in) thickness. However, this relaxation does not apply to a wall separating two dwellings (as in a semi-detached or terraced house), or between homes within a building (as in a block of flats).

In measuring the above dimensions, no allowance is to be made for the thickness of any fireback, or any material between the appliance and the fireplace recess.

The Pre-cast Fire Chamber

One of the simplest ways of equipping a house with a fireplace is to install a prefabricated fire-chamber. Most chimney manufacturers make a fire-chamber to fit their own system, but these flues are generally flexible enough to be adapted to fit any other manufactured flue series.

This pre-cast chamber is made of a reinforced, expanded, mineral-aggregate concrete. It comes in two models, one suitable for open fires, the other to accept closed stoves. Space is available in both models to accommodate back-boilers. These chambers are composed of a sequence of moulded concrete slabs, tongued and grooved, to be fitted together with cement or fire-clay. The speed of assembly is governed by the time taken for the cement to stabilise and can be accomplished in only a few minutes. Only the weight of the slabs may be an inhibitant. The assembled weight of the open-fire model is 369kg (812lb), and that of the closed stove model, with its heavy reinforced lintel, is 452kg (994lb). Some individual slabs weigh over 50kg (110lb).

Erection is started by cementing the base slab to the top surface of the constructional hearth. Thereafter, the slabs are fitted together, tongues into grooves, and cemented.

Wood fires can be lit on the base slab without any additional protection. Solid-fuel fires require a free-standing fire-basket or grate.

The side slabs can easily be cut or drilled in order to take hot-water central heating connections.

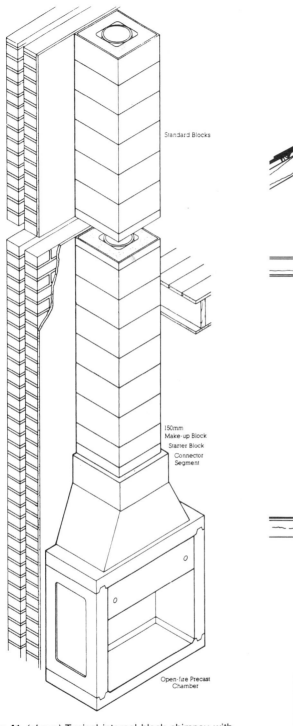

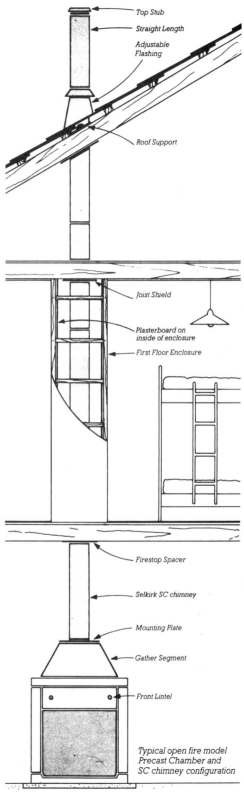

Standard Blocks

150mm
Make-up Block
Starter Block
Connector
Segment

Open-fire Precast
Chamber

Fig 41 *(above)* Typical internal block chimney with pre-cast fire chamber

Fig 42 *(right)* Pre-cast fire chamber showing typical installation

Top Stub
Straight Length
Adjustable Flashing
Roof Support
Joist Shield
Plasterboard on inside of enclosure
First Floor Enclosure
Firestop Spacer
Selkirk SC chimney
Mounting Plate
Gather Segment
Front Lintel

Typical open fire model Precast Chamber and SC chimney configuration

89

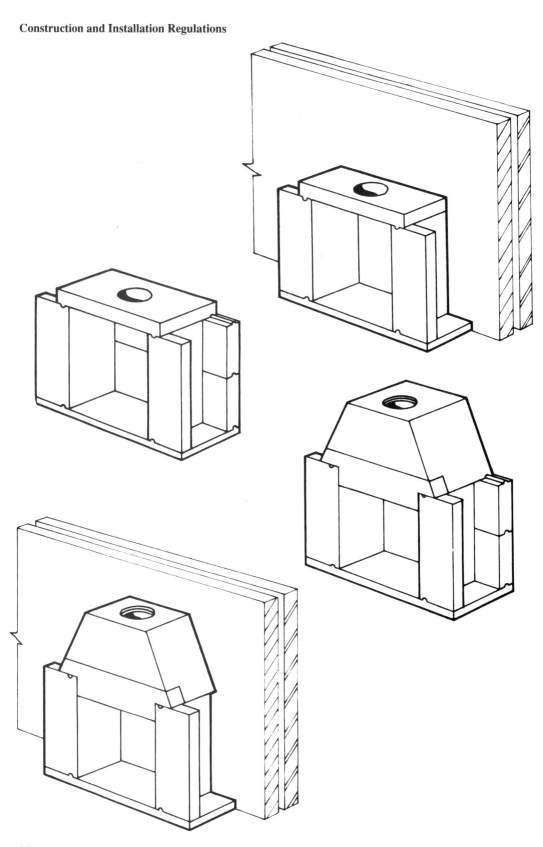

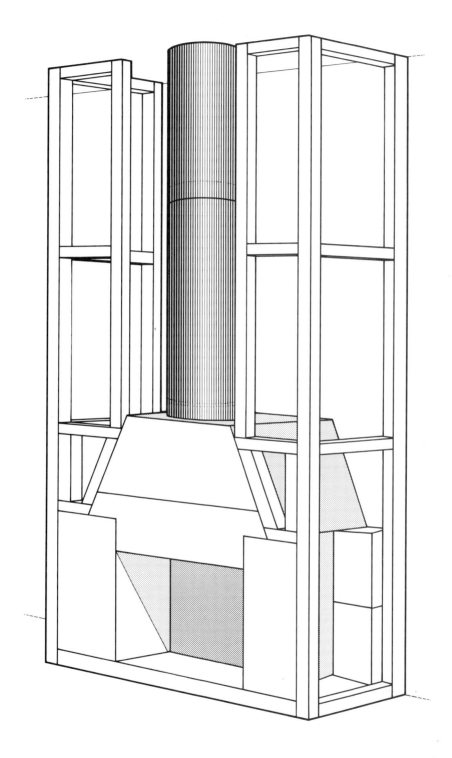

Fig 43 Parkachest prefabricated fire chambers *(left)* showing typical installation *(above)*; it would be fitted with a constructional hearth

91

Each of the chambers is stressed to bear a load of 6 tonnes. In tests, loads of over 10 tonnes have been supported. It is estimated that the weight of the heaviest concrete flues, rising to a height of 1m (3ft 3^1/2in) above ridge-pole height of a typical three-bedroomed semi-detached house, should not generally exceed 4 tonnes. The front of the chamber can be and decorated with one of the hundreds of proprietary fireplace designs on the market.

Both models conform to building regulations and can be installed anywhere with a minimum 50mm (2in) air-gap separation from adjacent walls and surrounds.

Chimneys and Flues

As with constructional hearths and fireplace recesses, chimneys and flue-pipes serving Class I appliances are required by building regulations to be constructed of unburnable material that is not materially affected by heat, the acid products of condensation (ie wood tar), or those of combustion (such as soot, etc). This material must be thick enough to withstand the effect of the most extreme heat as occurs, for example, during a chimney fire. Equally, it must be thick enough to prevent any part of the building being ignited by the fire's heat.

All Class I appliances must be connected to an adequate flue. No two fireplaces or stoves may be connected to the same chimney or flue.

Free-standing Stove Regulations

If you have decided to install a free-standing stove, there is a final range of building regulations requirements with which you must comply. They concern the safe distances between the stove case and any possible inflammable material.

Wherever you have chosen to place your constructional hearth (assuming it is not in a fireplace recess), you must make sure that any wall or partition within a distance of 150mm (6in) from the edge of the hearth is made of solid, unburnable material at least 75mm (3in) thick and to a height of not less than 1.2m (48in) above the top surface of the hearth.

In addition, measured horizontally, if any part of the back or sides of the stove case is within 150mm (6in) of the wall, then that wall must be made of solid unburnable material that is at least 75mm (3in) thick from floor level to a height of 300mm (12in) above the top of the stove.

Finally, should any part of the back or sides of the stove or heater be within 50mm (2in) of the wall (ie closer than the case quoted above), then the wall must be made of solid unburnable material at least 200mm (8in) thick from floor level to a height of 300mm (12in) above the top of the heating appliance.

Opening the Fireplace

In many old houses, particularly those over a century old, fireplaces have been blocked off. It takes some detective work to uncover them. Ludicrous though this may seem, it is a sensible idea to count the number of chimneys appearing above the roof, and trace each back to its source. Work on the basis that there must be at least one chimney to each fireplace.

Quite often a fireplace will be hidden behind some later work. If more than one fireplace is connected to a chimney, apart from it being illegal, working efficiency is greatly diminished. Suppose a fire is burning in a grate and the flue to which that grate is connected is linked also to another hearth elsewhere. A fire burns well by pulling fresh air into itself. If, at the same time, the rise of its fire-gas is pulling air through another fireplace (possibly one that is not housing a blazing fire), then air is being sucked into the chimney through the second fireplace and not through the one that is burning, which thereby burns with only half its proper vigour. (Eighteenth- and nineteenth-century builders often knew as little about the finer points of working fires as do their twentieth-century contemporaries).

Every generation, it seems, has its reasons for concealing fireplaces. It may have been just a change in life-style, as in the case of the modern owners who plasterboard over an entire wall, hiding everything, including the fireplace. Sometimes, there were reasons of economy; for instance, there was a fireplace tax for a time. The fireplace (possibly Victorian) will prove to be impossibly small with a capacity of no more than three or four decent-sized pieces of coal, as if some owner felt a desperate urge to save on fuel. This removed, there often appears another behind it, and another behind that, exposing a gradient of fireplace size. The more fireplaces discovered in this way, the older the house. These changes seem to arise at roughly fifty-year intervals, suggesting that a four-fireplace house (one behind another behind the next) is about two centuries old.

The exact nature of the excavations now involved will depend on the age of the house and the original use of the fire. A large chimney-breast may have been plastered over. Its presence could suggest the original use of the room as a kitchen or communal room. There may be a large, deeply recessed fireplace with a brick archway up to inglenook proportions and possibly a bread-oven.

Once the obstructions have been removed – plasterboard, previous fireplaces, brick-work, etc – it is necessary to check if the chimney will draw. Indeed, if there is any easy access through to the old chimney (ie by removing just a single brick if the closure was by a single layer of bricks), then it is very useful to light a taper or small candle and hold it to the opening. If the flame can be seen to be 'pulled' toward the hole, then the chimney is drawing properly (ie it is air-tight within the house and open to the exterior so that there is no obstruction to a column of air rising up it). When the flame is not 'pulled', further investigations are necessary. There is absolutely no point in proceeding with any further work until the chimney can be made to draw.

The next step may be a visual inspection. Much depends on the chimney size. In the instance suggested here, the removal of four fireplaces would suggest that the base of the chimney is large enough for the installer to push through and look directly up it. The width and height of the chimney terminal or top, outside, may also indicate if this is possible. If a clear view of the sky can be gained, there is no serious obstruction.

When the fireplace is not large enough, or there are bends in the chimney flue, to obtain a clear view it may be worth while to call the chimney sweep. His brushes can easily remove a temporary obstruction, for example, a brick that has fallen from the inner wall of the chimney and lodged in a bend. (This may also indicate that the chimney needs some remedial attention, for instance, relining with liquid cement (see pp 167–8)

If, despite an absence of obstructions, the chimney still will not draw, climb to the top of the chimney and partly close it with a piece of tile. Ignite a smoke pellet in the fireplace and check from floor to ceiling on each floor (or up the full height of the chimney if it is outside the house) to see if smoke is escaping. A serious crack in the chimney wall will prevent the flue from working properly.

Finally, ensure adequate air is drawn into the room where the fireplace is to be restored, to replace fire-gas rising up the chimney.

Any further difficulty may suggest more extensive investigations (see pp 120–22 and 132) or that it could be easier and quicker to ignore the old chimney and build a modern prefabricated unit.

Chimney Regulations

Factors governing the working of a chimney are more complex than is commonly supposed, and the building regulations are equally elaborate, so that no more than a general summary is possible here.

The term 'chimney' in the regulations indicates any part of the structure of a building forming any part of a flue other than a flue-pipe. An 'insulated metal chimney' comprises a flue lining, non-burnable thermal insulation and a metal outer casing.

When a chimney serving a Class I appliance (see p 87), is built as a separate building (ie not physically attached to the main structure), the building regulations which apply to it are Heat producing appliances J1/2/3 Approved Document J.

Chimneys constructed before 1 February 1966 may not conform in all respects with the recommendation of this Approved Document. Where this is the case and there is no obvious indication that the chimney is unsatisfactory it may be considered as satisfying the requirement.

General Requirements

Air supply: J1. Heat producing appliances shall be so installed that there is an adequate supply of air to them for combustion and for the efficient working of any flue-pipe or chimney.

Discharge of products of combustion: J2. Heat producing appliances shall have adequate provision for the discharge of the products of combustion to the outside air.

Protection of buildings: J3. Heat producing appliances and flue-pipes shall be so installed, and fireplaces and chimneys shall be so constructed, as to reduce to a reasonable level the risk of the building catching fire in consequence of their use.

The rules lay down that the chimney and flue-pipes must be constructed of non-burnable material, thick enough and stable enough to withstand the effects of heat, condensates and combustion products. It should not be possible for any part of the building to catch alight from the heat of the chimney. All the flue-pipes must be suitably placed and shielded to prevent this.

There must be a gap of at least 200mm (8in) between a chimney and any burnable material.

When a chimney is built using block construction (see pp 135–49), it is permissible to have burnable insulating material between the inner and outer wall.

Flue-pipes must be properly supported and must discharge their smoke to the exterior or into a chimney and thence to the exterior. Each flue must have an opening for cleaning, fitted with an air-tight door or cover made of non-burnable material.

There must be an adequate air supply from the dwelling into the flue for a full burning rate to be sustained and for the smoke to rise up into, and be discharged from, the flue (see pp 117–18).

In general, a flue serving any Class I appliance may only collect the smoke from that one appliance. There are , however, certain exceptions to this rule. For example, two solid-fuel stoves may feed into the same flue if both are mounted back to back in the same room. This arises when two rooms are knocked into one, leaving a central pillar with a stove installed on each of the two opposite sides. In such a case, each must be a closed stove and the two appliances must have a total rated heat output below 45Kw.

As will be seen in the section on flue terminals or cowls (pp 107 and 122–3), the placing of the flue outlet relative to the roof is vital for the efficient working of the fire. The flue top must be at least 1m (3ft 3$\frac{1}{2}$in) above the highest point of contact between it and the roof. If there are windows or skylights in the roof then the flue top must be 1m (3ft 3$\frac{1}{2}$in) above any one of these that is less than 2.3m (7ft 6in) away from the flue when measured horizontally.

Certain requirements are laid down for chimney liners in flues connected to Class I appliances (see below). Clay liners must conform to Building Standard 1181/1971. An acceptable alternative is to use rebated and socketed flue-pipe linings made of kiln-burnt aggregate and high alumina cement. (This is a regulation that affects the manufacturer of chimney-flue systems, but it is as well for the householder to know about it as he is ultimately held to be responsible for every installation in his house.)

Clay-pipe flue liners must also have a resistance to acid attack that accords with British Standard 65/1981. Insulated metal linings must conform to British Standard 4543. In both cases manufacturers must be able to confirm that their products satisfy these determinations.

When erecting a chimney-flue system, care must be taken that no joints between sections of flue-pipe occur within the thickness of any wall, floor, roof or ceiling. There must be ready access for inspection or replacement of the flue-pipe throughout its length.

Where old large chimneys survive it is possible to run modern, narrow flue-pipes up through them. However, wherever this is done there must be preserved a minimum of 100mm (4in) thickness of non-burnable material between any such flues mounted in the same chimney

In the case where a chimney separates two houses, there must be at least 200mm (8in) of non-burnable material between the chimney and the adjoining house, excluding air gaps.

While a flue throat – immediately above the fire – may be temporarily or permanently constricted for the purpose of fire-gas control, elsewhere along the length of the flue connected to a Class I appliance the cross-section of the flue must not be less than the equivalent of a circle of 175mm (7in) diameter.

When insulated metal chimneys are to be installed, their run upwards must be planned so that any angle away from the vertical does not exceed 45°, except where necessary at the base or bottom end, to connect the chimney to the stove.

There are restrictions on the passing of a Class I flue-pipe through any roof space, floor, internal wall or partition. In essence, what the regulations say is that an uninsulated flue-pipe is forbidden passage but that, suitably protected and with insulated collars giving the necessary separation, such an installation is permitted.

There is no restriction on passing a flue-pipe through an external wall or through a roof provided the regulations regarding insulation and separation from burnable substances are observed – ie it must be separated by three times the external diameter of the pipe from any burnable material, or separated by 200mm (8in) from burnable material provided it (the flue) is totally enclosed in a metal or asbestos cement sleeve.

The cross-sectional area of any flue must not be less than the cross-section of the outlet to which it is connected.

Throughout these regulations it can be taken that the 'deemed to satisfy' provisions apply and are not mandatory. In other words, the builder or installer can use some other mode of construction provided the local authority building inspector can be satisfied that it is a satisfactory mode and complies with the spirit of the regulations.

Finally, and in general, it is a fundamental principle running throughout all these requirements that any flue-pipe must be placed sufficiently far away from burnable materials as to prevent the ignition of that material, or else a non-burnable shield must be interposed between the flue-pipe and the burnable material.

Chimney Construction
External Chimney

It can be reasonably assumed that any house lacking a chimney is almost certainly of modern construction. There are, of course. rare exceptions and it can happen that an older house with chimneys, has none in a desired or convenient position. That being the case, the decision must be taken as to where the new chimney should be placed. The first consideration is whether it should be built inside or outside the house.

Apart from the initial task of cutting a hole to carry the flue connection through the base of the house wall, external construction is by far the simplest, and therefore the first method to be described here.

Placing the fireplace inside the house is one of the major considerations (see p 15), but matching it is the possible existence of an outside wall uncluttered by any pipes, gutters or other attachments.

It is desirable (see p 101) to have a clean, straight rise up to the roof, with the possibility of tying the chimney into the wall and extending it to a height of at least 1m (3ft 3½in) above ridge-pole height. If there are neighbouring roofs even higher, or if there are tall trees or any other form of obstruction likely to cause swirls and down-draughts around the chimney top, then it may be desirable to carry the chimney even higher, but not so high as to risk destabilisation in high winds.

The exact site for the chimney having been decided, the first task is to provide an adequate foundation for it. This is often not given enough attention. It must be remembered that a plain chimney extending upwards to a height of 4–5m (13–16ft) can easily weigh up to 4 tonnes. If a sufficiently strong foundation is not provided, the base of the chimney can collapse under this weight and the entire structure pull away from the wall, leaving all the hard work to be done over again.

It cannot be emphasised enough that the work involved in laying the foundation must not be skimped. A foundation must be dug to a depth equal to that for the house itself, and certainly to below frost level. This can be filled with a mix of gravel and cement, or some similar weight-supporting infilling mix, up to soil level. The top surface must then be levelled carefully and left to dry out, preferably for a week, allowing the filling to both dry and settle. Some account of the weather should be taken at this stage. Continuous cold, driving rain is not helpful. The construction of a chimney foundation must conform to building regulations (see pp 92, 100, 172).

Matching preparations must now be made inside the house where there are two possible arrangements. The fireplace can be a free-standing unit in front of the wall itself, or it may be recessed into the wall. In the former case, at a point behind and above where the fireplace, with or without stove unit, is to be placed, a hole must be cut through the wall, angled to carry the connecting flue-pipe upwards at an angle of 45°. (It is permissible to have a horizontal connection from the fireplace through to the exterior. A short run of horizontal pipe is not going to reduce materially the working performance of the fire, provided arrangements are made for it to be easily cleared of soot and /or tar. An angled pipe, however, is better.)

If the fireplace is to be recessed into the wall, its place against the wall should be marked and a token recess commenced. A preliminary drilling through the wall should be made to ensure that the external construction will marry with that inside the house

When the fireplace inside the house is a free-standing one, then a solid chimney support of concrete blocks can be built against the outside wall. This can take the form of a U-plan section of blocks against the wall, filled with hard rubble or compacted hardcore which is well bedded down.

It is important during this construction, at every level upwards from the foundation, to check carefully that the blocks are laid horizontally and are plumbed vertically to the wall. This construction is carried up to whatever height the flue-pipe connection from inside the house will emerge.

Where the fireplace in the house is to be recessed, it will probably prove that the rear of the fireplace chamber or chest will project beyond the outside wall. A U-plan section of concrete blocks, large enough to contain this, is built, leaving a gap between the rear of the fire-chest and the concrete blocks. This gap is to be filled with hard rubble, as before.

From now onwards, the external constructional methods for both types of installation are identical. (Only one minor variation of the internal building remains to be described.)

A reinforced-concrete lintel is laid on a liberal bed of mortar across the top of the constructed chimney base. (A suitable mortar mix is one part cement, two parts lime, nine parts fine sand.) The purpose of the lintel is to provide a support base for the chimney and an air connection through from the fireplace.

The external chimney foundation can now be squared or tapered off to receive the first chimney block. This should be one of the open-sided blocks. ie a three-sided U-plan block, the fourth side of which is to be occupied by a metal soot door. This door will make it an easy task to pass a flue brush upwards to clean the full run of the chimney, and downwards and inwards to clear the flue-pipe connection into the fireplace.

Mention must be made here of the two possible ways of creating a fireplace on the constructional hearth. The first may seem the simpler method, but it has attendant difficulties where a horizontal pipe is fitted. (This information is modified by the new building regulation that no horizontal flue connection from the stove or fire-chest through to the base of the chimney may exceed 150mm (6in).) Using either bricks or concrete blocks, build two 230mm (9in) pillars on the constructional hearth, a suitable distance apart to accommodate whatever grate or closed stove has been chosen to be installed. These pillars should enclose a space deep enough to contain both the grate or stove and a protective back wall to be built in front of the existing house wall. Average dimensions would be about 1,000mm (3ft 3$\frac{1}{2}$in) high, 800mm (2ft 8in) wide and 340mm (13ft $\frac{1}{2}$in) deep.

At the appropriate height on each pillar, left and right 'gathers' should be built into the structure. These are to provide a smooth fire-gas feed upwards into the lintel and flue-pipe and so up the exterior chimney. However, for proper security, this arrangement requires two lintels, one inside and one outside the house, which results in an expensive and somewhat complex combination to furnish the necessary support for the chimney.

A much simpler arrangement is to recess a pre-fabricated fire-chest (see pp 145–151) into the house wall or immediately in front of it (depending on the thickness of the wall) so that a flue-pipe connection can run from it directly into the exterior flue. In that case, only a single support lintel is needed on the outer wall.

In many regards, once the interior and exterior chimney base construction has been completed, the remainder of the operation is fairly simple and largely repetitive. However, one difficulty remains to be circumvented. Individual prefabricated chimney-flue blocks weigh approximately 20kg (44lb) each. This is not a convenient or comfortable weight for most people to lift into position, especially as it will be necessary to have some means of climbing to the top of the construction as it progresses. It would be dangerous even to attempt to use a ladder as both hands are needed to hold the block, leaving no means of supporting oneself on the ladder.

It might be possible to set up some simple form of block and tackle which would take the sting out of the lifting problem. However, having a heavy block swinging at the end of a long rope would be most awkward to control. In addition, there might be a danger that the block could swing free and hit the person on the ladder, if not the ladder itself.

Although tiresome and taking up additional construction time, the most stable and satisfactory remedy is to erect metal scaffolding. This can generally be rented by the day and is not difficult to erect. The metal pipes are held together by metal collars, each secured by a screw. Such scaffolding can be erected safely to any height required in a house chimney erection. Furthermore, it is quite easy to build the scaffold with planks inserted, and secured firmly in place, at easy step heights, making it possible to climb safely holding a heavy block between the hands.

With the exterior foundation built, the connection with the fireplace inside the house made and the exterior lintel laid in place, construction of the chimney can now begin.

A liberal bed of mortar is put down on the lintel top and the first block is centred on it. It must be levelled horizontally and checked for vertical alignment. Surplus mortar must be removed from both outside and inside the block. (This first block is mounted on top of the U-section block already laid, and containing a soot door. Alternatively, depending on the configuration of any particular installation, the soot door unit may be built in a few courses higher up, if that is where the flue from the interior makes its

connection, especially if it is angled at 45°.)

Some types of chimney blocks have moulded into them pegs and slots, the one fitting into the other, to ensure that each block is correctly fitted. Other systems have a projecting rim on one block to mate with a recessed shoulder on its neighbour. These must always be connected with the projecting rim pointing upwards so that it overlays the recessed shoulder above it. This is so that the interior surface of the flue remains as smooth as possible. For the same reason it is important to remove any surplus mortar form the inner surface of the flue and make sure that there are no projections or protuberances. Anything of this nature can impede the rise of the hot fire-gas and become the possible cause of tar or soot being deposited.

In addition to bonding the chimney to the house wall at every level with mortar, it is also important to 'tie in' the chimney to the wall with metal ties of some type. Each manufacturer will have recommended ties and specified intervals at which these should be placed. Among the simplest are non-corroding stainless steel wire ties usually inserted at about 750mm (30in) vertical intervals.

At some point the rise of the chimney is going to make contact with the roof. If the chimney is being built up an end wall, there will be an overhang of tiles or other roof covering. These must be carefully cut back to allow the chimney to rise up past them.

When the chimney level is clear of, and above, the roof line or ridge-pole height, the gap between the chimney and the roof must be sealed with flashing. Some prefer to seal this with mortar or cement, but a better way is to use a proprietary brand of lead sheeting which is soft enough to be bent or moulded by hand and is completely impervious to weathering. Such sheets can also be cut easily to shape.

The essential point about flashings is that they must prevent rain water running down between two surfaces or into any gap, no matter how small, and so penetrating the house's anti-damp defences and undermining the flashing's protection.

The lead sheets should·be cut so that they lie flat over the tiles adjacent to the chimney, each sheet lapping over the one next to it. There should be an overlap of about 25mm

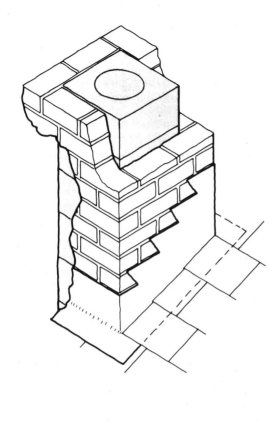

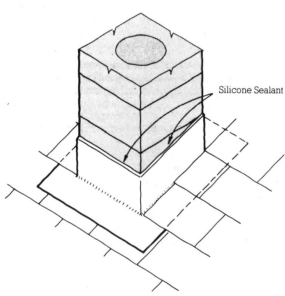

Silicone Sealant

Fig 44 Selkirk chimney flashing

(lin). These sheets can then be bent or worked by hand so that they turn and run flat up the outside wall of the chimney on each of the three sides where the chimney abuts the roof.

Finally, the edges of the flashing can then be bonded onto the side of the chimney with waterproof sealant (there are a number of proprietary brands available from builders' merchants and ironmongers or hardware shops.)

For decorative effect, the side edge of the flashing is sometimes cut in steps, especially where the chimney is built of brick. This, however, seems to add little to the flashing's protective effect and makes the final job of creating a totally waterproof seal between the roof and chimney that more difficult.

The chimney can now be built on up to its finished height which must be not less than 1m (3ft 3 ½in) above ridge-pole height and may be somewhat higher if local circumstances dictate that (see pp 126-8).

The chimney is then finished off with a small capping laid on a generous bed of mortar, again making sure that the inner flue surface is smooth and free of obstruction. Any minor projection from the flue wall will have a much stronger effect on the flow of flue gas at this height than it will have lower down where the gas is hotter and rising more powerfully.

The possibility of adding a cowl or terminal of one type or another will be examined on pp 107–113).

Internal Chimney

Inevitably, the construction of the internal chimney starts with an adequate foundation. Various considerations have directed the choice of location for the fireplace. One of these will have been the nature of the foundations on which the house is built. Some of the smaller, modern estate houses seem to have no more than a plain concrete raft to support them. If this is the case, then the first task of the householder intending to install a fireplace is to provide a proper foundation for the chimney. The raft will need to be deepened below where the chimney is to be placed.

Older homes with wooden flooring will have an air gap below the house. Enough of the flooring can be temporarily removed for a pit to be dug down to foundation (ie frost-free) level and filled with a mix of hard rubble and cement. Allow at least a week in hot dry weather, and longer in cold, wet conditions for this to dry out.

The foundation is built up to floor level and forms the base of the required constructional hearth. The floor can now be restored. In just the same way as has already been described in the section on the constructional hearth (see pp 85–8), some type of placement is prepared, depending on there variety of heating apparatus that will eventually occupy it. It may be the home owner's intention to have nothing more elaborate than a plain grate on which to burn an open solid fuel or wood fire. (Log fires burn quite satisfactorily on a grate of fire-bars; a solid bed of wood-ash is not essential.) Side pillars with a back wall and 'gathers' will be enough for this, topped by a lintel.

A free-standing closed stove or boiler unit needs only a projecting apron of constructional hearth around its base. A back - or top-mounted flue (ie one running either vertically or horizontally from the stove) can run directly into a connection to the base of the flue.

Inset or hole-in-the-wall fires need to be built into the wall either by recessing to the required depth, or a recess can be created by building the wall forward by two or three layers of bricks or building blocks.

These are just a few of the installation variables that may be considered. All will be concluded with a supporting lintel above the fireplace, chamber or chest, that will form a support for the 4 tonnes weight of the chimney.

The first chimney block is mounted on the lintel with a generous layer of mortar. Other blocks follow in sequence to just below ceiling height. Make sure the blocks are placed so that the inner flue surface is smooth. Check at each level that the blocks are horizontal and plumbed vertical to the wall.

Once the mortar is totally dry, the chimney-pillar or breast can be plastered, brick clad or dry lined, according to taste.

The second course above the lintel can be an open-sided or U-plan block so that an air-tight soot door can be fitted. This provides a useful alternative to sweeping the chimney through the air-tight stove, which is sometimes awkward, involving the removal of the upper butterfly valve air control.

The next stage of the operation involves some semi-skilled carpentry. The ceiling and upper flooring must now be cut back so that the chimney can pass through. With some careful planning in the placing of the stove and chimney, it may be necessary to cut only one joist. This is desirable because the joist is a main structural support for the floor. However many joists need to be cut, their ends must be boxed in to the adjacent joists so that a firm support into the wall is retained. A minimum air gap of 50mm (2in) must be retained between any structural timbers and the outer surface of the chimney. Skirtingboards and floorboards can be run right up to the chimney, although in practice it is preferable even here to leave a narrow gap of perhaps 10mm ($^3/_8$in). With the joists, floorboards and skirting cut back, the chimney can be built up above the level of the upper flooring.

Once the upper ceiling is reached, there can be a pause in the upward construction. Again, once entirely dry, this upper section of chimney can be decorated. This is a good opportunity to do the plastering which, being a messy business, should be done while the house is in a messy condition anyway.

The same procedure is followed to take the chimney up into the roof space as for rising up through the upper floor. It is, however, important that the main cross-beam supports to the roof are not broken into or disturbed, and the rise of the chimney should have been chosen with this consideration in mind.

There must be a minimum gap of 50mm (2in) between the outer surface of the chimney and any structural timber. For complete safety, a small gap should be retained between the ceiling plasterboard and the chimney, this gap to be filled with asbestos sheet substitute.

Enough of the roof surface (tiles, slates or sheet cladding) must be removed to allow the chimney to rise up above the ridge-pole. It is best to undertake this work when there is some prospect of dry weather for a few days, otherwise a precautionary temporary covering of plastic sheeting must be available with some means to secure it against wind and rain.

A wooden frame should now be mounted against the chimney surface, following the line of the roof through which it is passing. If the chimney emerges through the ridge-pole, the wooden frame will have an inverted 'V' shape. If it comes out through the roof itself, it will have a plain slope. The roof covering is restored to be level with this wooden frame which then becomes the base support for the lead flashings necessary at this roof chimney junction. (See pp 97–8 for sealing with flashing.)

If the chimney is to have a plain cement or pebble-dash finish, then no additional components are needed other than the necessary number of chimney blocks to rise to whatever height above the ridge-pole is thought to be desirable for the best performance of the chimney, bearing in mind any local obstructions such as higher roofs, trees or sharp rises in the terrain itself.

A small capping is placed on a bed of mortar 10mm ($\frac{1}{2}$in) thick, the flashings are mortared in position and the main constructional task is completed.

However, the householder may want to clad the chimney from the roof upwards with bricks to match the rest of the house. This requires a corbel, ie a square support section to be built into the chimney structure between blocks at the lowest level at which the chimney emerges from the roof. The corbel will protrude beyond the line of the blocks and offers a ledge to support a single skin of bricks. These are built. into position, the roof is restored to mate with them, the flashings are fitted and mortared into place and the chimney top is finished off with a large capping bedded into a thick layer of mortar. Because the corbel extends beyond the chimney blocks it may be desirable to brace it with a half brick cemented underneath it at each corner.

These notes describe a basic constructional programme and minor variations that occur between the different designs and recommendations of different manufacturers. Illustrations showing these differences are included here so that comparisons can be made.

External Stainless Steel Chimney

The initial preparation is identical with that for building a block chimney (see pp 135–149). Proper foundations must be prepared below the constructional hearth. A placing for the stove or grate must be laid out either with brick or slab pillars or a pre-fabricated fire-chest or chamber.

It is a useful precaution before making final dispositions to check with the local authority building inspector the precise local interpretations of various advisory precepts in building regulations. These vary in detail from authority to authority and it is, of course, the local requirements that must be complied with. Strictly, a pro forma building regulations approval must be secured for the installation in any case, although again, the precise implementation of this varies from place to place.

Although there is less of a weight problem with stainless steel chimneys than there is with block constructions, the problem remains the same. Stainless steel chimney sections weigh less per metre than do block chimneys, but as they are supplied in longer lengths, the householder still finds that there is a fairly substantial load to be lifted. Therefore, rented scaffolding will need to be erected outside the house up along the line of the proposed chimney (consult *Yellow Pages* for building equipment hire firms).

Once the scaffolding is in position it is helpful to drop a plumb line down from the highest point on the roof where the chimney will emerge. From this line, score a line right down the wall as a guide to holding the correct placing when putting the chimney sections in place.

Stainless steel chimney sections come in various diameters and the correct size must be chosen. The chimney diameter must not be less than that of the flue exit pipe coming from the stove being installed. For open fires, 200mm (8in) is the generally accepted minimum diameter.

The chimney height will, of course, be conditioned by the type and size of house against which it is to be built, but for efficient fire working it should not be less than 3.6m (12ft) for single-storey houses and 4.3m (14ft) for two-storey houses.

Because of the weight of the chimney, its base must always be supported. Prefabricated fire-chests or chambers are often stressed to support a load of 6 tonnes. The weight of even the most substantial chimney is not going to exceed 4 tonnes.

With offset installations, ie where the flue connection runs horizontally from the back of the stove into the base of the chimney, at least one manufacturer supplies a telescopic floor support. This can be adjusted to the height above the floor and then locked into position. The horizontal run must not exceed 150mm (6in).

Load-bearing lintels can be included in the structure at any height from just above the fire-chamber to just below the ground-floor ceiling.

Where a flue-pipe connection runs at an angle (about 45°) through the wall, then external support brackets can be used to support and brace the chimney to the wall. Care should be taken that the wall is strong enough to support this load.

For each stainless steel chimney system there will be some type of locking arrangement between sections. It goes without saying that each section must be securely locked into the next. If there are ceramic liners, then the manufacturer's joint sealant must be applied to both ceramic end faces before the sections are secured together. External locking bands are also supplied on some models (ie Selkirk). There are grooves moulded into the metal surface into which these fit.

With each particular system there will be a right and wrong direction in which the sections are to be connected. Generally, the means of locking will indicate which is right and which is wrong. The reason for this arrangement is that there should be an internal mask, covering the joint between sections and so providing a smooth surface in the chimney that will not cause friction losses in the rapid flow of the hot fire-gas.

For chimneys serving Class I appliances (see p 87), apart from the flue-pipe connection at the chimney base, it is not permissible to have any bend away from the vertical of more than 30° (or a bend away from the horizontal of no less than 60°). Thus, if the chimney is being carried up a side wall of the house, there will probably be no need for any deviation, but if it is being carried up a front wall, then it may be necessary to bend it around guttering. This can be done easily using standard units.

An intermediate wall-bracket support is used to tie in the chimney to the wall at a convenient height just below the gutter. A 30° elbow unit is fitted into the topmost chimney section using the same methods of locking adjacent chimney sections. One or more standard chimney sections are then added to carry the chimney up to its designated height.

These general notes apply to almost all chimney systems of this type available in the UK. However, certain points of detail apply to some systems and not others. For example, some manufacturers give access to the chimney for cleaning and inspection by incorporating a tee-section at the base of an offset flue. This allows the chimney to be swept if access through the stove is difficult. With this arrangement it is vital to remember always to replace the tee-plug or cap or the air 'pull' through the fire will be severely diminished. Another method is to fit an inspection door section in the flue-pipe immediately above the stove (in a short vertical rise section) before it bends to pass through the wall.

Wherever a flue-pipe passes through a wall to the exterior, as in an angled connection to the base of a flue. Selkirk recommends that a wall sleeve be used. This is to stabilise the flue-pipe in the wall, and across the insulation cavity if there is one, against thermal movement (ie expansion and contraction) and to provide additional support to the external chimney. Selkirk also specifies that no run of chimney must exceed a vertical height of 10m (32ft 11in).

All systems require the external chimney to be secured to the wall by ties or brackets at regular intervals of about 750mm (2ft 6in).

Internal Stainless Steel Chimney

The primary installation requirements are identical to those for an external chimney – load-bearing foundation beneath the constructional hearth and an inbuilt placing for the stove (see pp 55 and 86).

If the stove is a free-standing unit, it will be quite usual to run a connecting pipe not exceeding 150mm (6in) horizontally from its rear and then vertically into the ceiling. One advantage of this arrangement is that on many stoves both a top and rear connection are provided. Where the rear connection is used, the top opening is closed with a cast metal heating or cooking plate, suitable for minor culinary use such as heating water or milk for hot drinks etc.

A stove standing in an alcove or inglenook will have a vertical connection running from its top surface.

Stainless steel chimney sections are supplied in various lengths, and these should be chosen so that no connecting joint between sections occurs within the space of a ceiling/floor or ceiling/roof.

Where the chimney passes through a ceiling/floor the specified separation from burnable material (ie 50mm (2in)) must be maintained.

An intermediate ceiling support must be used where the flue passes through a ceiling/floor. This is no more than a pair of matching collars that slide over the flue and secure to the joists. If there is less than the necessary 50mm (2in) gap between the flue-pipe and surrounding joists, then a joist shield must be used. This consists of a protective sleeve with two fire-stop plates, top and bottom.

The building technique is the same as that for the external installation. The appropriate sealant is applied to the end surfaces of the chimney sections and to any ceramic or other liner that may be included. A common form of securing device is a locking band incorporating a toggle catch. Once two sections are secured, a check should be made that the inner wall of the flue is smooth. Any projecting sealing compound should be wiped away before it sets. Note that wherever toggles are used, these usually project a short distance beyond the outside diameter of the flue. If there is a tight fit on one side, the flue should be rotated to a position where there is space enough to take the toggle catch. This projection is usually no more than about 12mm ($\frac{1}{2}$in).

Where it is not convenient to install a load-bearing lintel above the stove – for example, in an inglenook – this can be built in at ceiling level to form a combined load-bearing ceiling support. This support distributes the chimney weight back down to the fire-chest and hearth, and sideways to the timber joists. The adjustable gimbal plates must be firmly fixed to the joists with at least 50mm (2in) screws all round. Gimbal plates consist of

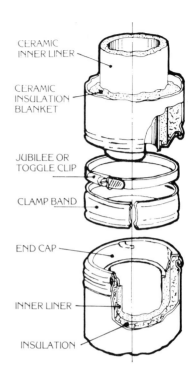

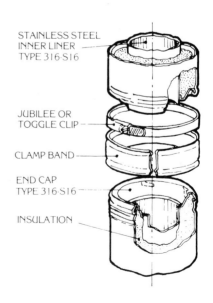

Fig 45 Insulated chimney components: ceramic *(top)*, and stainless steel

two horizontally mounted support brackets with a rotatable support ring between them. This allows support to be secured from angled timbers while retaining a horizontal position for the support ring around the vertical chimney flue.

Many of these types of chimney go into older houses, few of which have anything approaching a standard configuration. Obviously, it is not possible in a book of this size and scope to describe every possible permutation and combination of installation arrangements and layouts, but there is now such a wide variety of different types of fixing components being marketed by different manufacturers, many of which are compatible between one range of products and another, that it is really only necessary to work out which bits and pieces are necessary to do the job required. In that basic planning it should be a cardinal rule that wherever there is a doubt, err on the side of safety by putting in two fixings where perhaps one might do.

One major manufacturer, Selkirk, lists thirty-four different components, each of them coming in a variety of sizes. These range from elbows, tees and adapter fittings to flashings for every type of situation, collars, sleeves, terminals, caps, tops; many kinds of support, telescopic models, tee supports, ceiling supports, base supports, roof supports; shields, bands, plates and rings, condensate collectors and a removal trap for condensation and soot.

Another manufacturer, Rite-Vent, includes adaptors, bends, offsets, insulated tees, wall sleeves, supports, bands, branches, roof plates, collars, flashings, coping caps, terminals, etc.

A further joist shield may be necessary where the flue rises from the top floor ceiling into the roof space. Thereafter, there are two possibilities. If the chimney – its route having been chosen to avoid roof timbers – is to rise vertically and emerge from the roof at the ridge-pole, a peak flashing can be used. This consists of a soft lead sleeve to which are attached flat plates at angles appropriate to that of the roof on which the installation is being made. Roof pitches of $9\frac{1}{2}°, 18\frac{1}{2}°, 26\frac{1}{2}°, 39\frac{1}{2}°$ and $45°$, are available. These are supplied with a storm collar and non-setting caulking compound.

The chimney can now be extended upwards by as many lengths as are necessary to reach the required height, which must be a minimum of 1m (3ft $3\frac{1}{2}$in) above ridge-pole height.

If the chimney is to be finished with brick cladding, a square chimney housing should be mounted on the flue at this point.

Before the chimney is finished off, it is a sensible precaution to make a smoke test. This need be no more elaborate than to light some screws of rubbish in the fireplace below. If the fire draws well, ie there is a steady rise of smoke from the chimney top, a strong 'draw' into the fireplace and with no smoke escaping back into the house, then the chimney can be finished off with a plain pot terminal. If there is not a good draw, it is possible there are down-draught problems. Possibly some adjacent roof is higher than the chimney terminal, or there may be tall trees nearby. With wind in a particular direction, air can spill from these down onto your chimney top, preventing the fire-gas smoke from escaping freely. These difficulties are discussed fully on pp 135–177.

If a vertical chimney-flue rise through the roof space is not possible, an elbow can be inserted above top ceiling level. This angles the flue to one side. Interior support brackets can be used to secure this angled section to any convenient main roof timber. Insertion of another angled elbow brings the chimney flue run back to the vertical. Sufficient roof tiles, slates or other coverings are removed to permit the flue to pass through. Its position is secured with a roof support. Then, as before, a roof flashing is placed over the flue and worked down to roof level. A storm collar is placed over it, the flashing sheets are worked by hand to fit the contours of the roof and are finished with caulking compound.

External Brick Chimney

There is very little difference in the construction procedures between brick and slab or block construction.

Preparation starts with a firm foundation below the constructional hearth. A stove or grate placing is built on the constructional hearth using bricks to form pillars. A hole is cut through the exterior wall for the flue

Fig 46 Isokern chimney components

440 x 440mm Single outer casing
Used to form outer casing for 200mm diameter single-flue DM chimneys, or up to 225mm diameter chimneys using standard system.

internal	external	height	weight
325 x 325mm	**440 x 440mm**	300mm	22kg

545 x 545mm Single outer casing
Used to form outer casing for 250mm or 300mm diameter single-flue DM chimneys.

internal	external	height	weight
430 x 430mm	**545 x 545mm**	300mm	37kg

440 x 800mm Double outer casing
Used to form outer casing for 200mm diameter twin-flue DM chimneys, or up to 225mm diameter twin-flue chimneys using standard system.

internal	external	height	weight
2 x 325 x 325mm	**440 x 800mm**	300mm	43kg

Starter flue block
Half-height inner liner for use as starter block to achieve staggered joint construction.

internal diameter	external	height	weight
200mm	310 x 310mm	150mm	6.5kg
250mm	430 x 430mm	150mm	12kg
300mm	430 x 430mm	150mm	7.5kg

Flue block
Full-height inner liner.

internal diameter	external	height	weight
200mm	310 x 310mm	300mm	13kg
250mm	430 x 430mm	300mm	24kg
300mm	430 x 430mm	300mm	15kg

Breach block
Three-wall outer casing designed to provide clean-out; used below flue entry. Flue block not required.

internal diameter	external	opening	height	weight
200mm	440 x 440mm	230 x 285mm	285mm	20kg
250mm	545 x 545mm	230 x 285mm	285mm	39kg
300mm	545 x 545mm	230 x 285mm	285mm	35kg

Clean-out block
Three-wall outer casing with soot door fitted; used below flue entry. Flue block not required.

internal diameter	external	height	weight
200mm	440 x 440mm	285mm	26kg
250mm	545 x 545mm	285mm	45kg
300mm	545 x 545mm	285mm	41kg

Access casings (in pairs)
Used in pairs (top/bottom) to create a DM outer casing with 220mm access (to suit 200mm) for 90° flue entry or clean-out.

internal	external	height	weight
325 x 325mm	**440 x 440mm**	300mm	20kg

Access flue block
Used in conjunction with the DM access casings to provide a 220mm diameter aperture for flue entry or clean-out.

internal diameter	external	height	weight
200mm	310 x 310mm	300mm	10kg

Casing ties
Stainless-steel ties supplied with masonry bolt and used to tie the outer casings back to the building structure.

Capping for rendered casing
For use with single DM casings and standard system as a capping to a rendered chimney stack only.

internal	external	height	weight
325 x 325mm	**570 x 570mm**	70mm	25kg
(for 440mm casing)			
420 x 420mm	**670 x 670mm**	70mm	30kg
(for 545 DM casing and 580mm standard casing)			

Capping for brickwork casing
For use with single DM casings and standard system as a capping to a brick-clad chimney only.

internal	external	height	weight
320 x 320mm	**810 x 810mm**	70mm	55kg
(for 440mm casing)			
420 x 420mm	**950 x 950mm**	70mm	80kg
(for 545mm DM casing and 580mm standard casing)			

Corbel for brickwork casing
For use with single DM casings and standard system to support brickwork.

internal	external	height	weight
325 x 325mm	**655 x 655mm**	75mm	57kg
(for 440mm casing)			
430 x 430mm	**795 x 795mm**	80mm	85kg
(for 545 DM casing)			

Corbel for double casing

internal	external	height	weight	
325 x 325mm	**655 x 1020mm**	75mm	74kg	(2 pieces)
(for 440 x 800mm casing)				

Offset corbel for brickwork casing
For use with 440 x 440mm single DM casings and standard system to support brickwork on three sides.

internal	external	height	weight
325 x 325mm	**655 x 560mm**	75mm	38kg

Offset block
Special 440mm DM casing used singly or in multiples to form an offset bend; offset dimension 85mm (30°). Designed to be used without a flue block.

internal diameter	external	height
200mm	440 x 570mm	150mm

Liner adaptor
Adaptor for connecting appliance flue pipe to 200mm diameter DM chimney.

internal	external	height
200mm	**310mm** across flats	75mm

Firechest
Used to construct fireplace or appliance recess. Modular height in units of 215mm; normally supplied to give a total height of 900mm.

internal (W x D x H) 700 x 340 x 900mm;
external 900 x 440 x 900mm. 100mm wall thickness;
215mm modular height.
weight 360kg

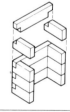

Gather/lintel unit
Used with firechest or brickwork to construct fireplace recess; will support total 1 tonne chimney weight. Supplied in two parts.

internal	external	height	weight
200 x 200mm	900 x 440mm	450mm	122kg
			(80kg + 42kg)

Raft lintel
Used with firechest or brickwork to construct appliance recess.

internal diameter	external (W x D x H)	weight
200mm	900 x 440 x 140mm	125kg

Support lintel
Used with standard system to reduce width of cladding brickwork above firechest or Featurefire whilst providing support; requires loadbearing brickwork below, at either end. Supplied in two parts. See DM system for description.

Adhesive Sealant
Flexible, corrosion and heat resistant sealant (fire cement) in 310ml cartridge.

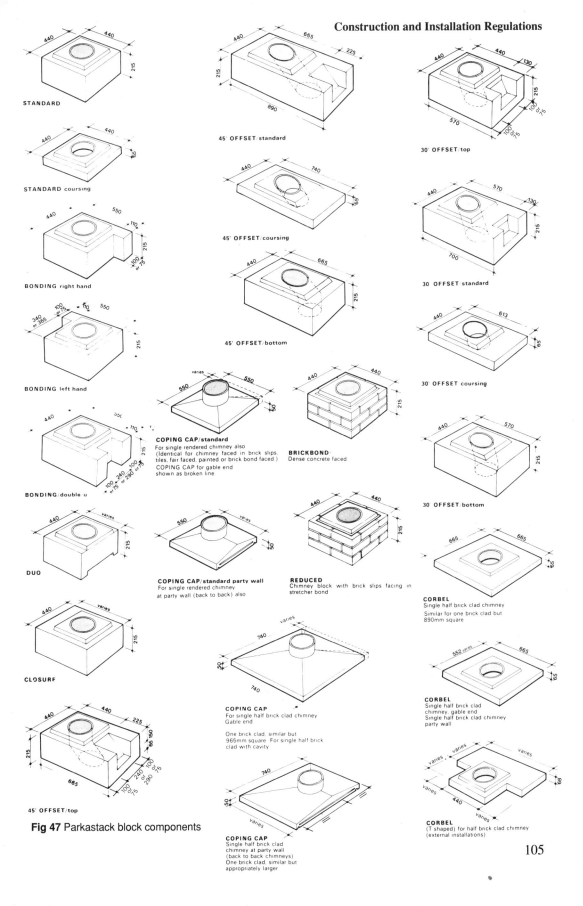

Fig 47 Parkastack block components

STANDARD

STANDARD coursing

BONDING right hand

BONDING left hand

BONDING/double u

DUO

CLOSURE

45° OFFSET/top

45° OFFSET/standard

45° OFFSET/coursing

45° OFFSET/bottom

COPING CAP/standard
For single rendered chimney also
(Identical for chimney faced in brick slips,
tiles, fair faced, painted or brick bond faced.)
COPING CAP for gable end
shown as broken line

COPING CAP/standard party wall
For single rendered chimney
at party wall (back to back) also

COPING CAP
For single half brick clad chimney
Gable end

One brick clad, similar but
965mm square. For single half brick
clad with cavity

COPING CAP
Single half brick clad
chimney at party wall
(back to back chimneys)
One brick clad, similar but
appropriately larger

BRICKBOND
Dense concrete faced

REDUCED
Chimney block with brick slips facing in
stretcher bond

30° OFFSET/top

30° OFFSET/standard

30° OFFSET coursing

30° OFFSET/bottom

CORBEL
Single half brick clad chimney
Similar for one brick clad but
890mm square

CORBEL
Single half brick clad
chimney, gable end
Single half brick clad chimney
party wall

CORBEL
(T shaped) for half brick clad chimney
(external installations)

105

Photo 67 Tudor Chimney Tops at Hampton Court

connection to be made.

Externally, instead of the prefabricated blocks, the chimney is built up with courses (ie layers) of bricks. Each layer should be staggered from the one below so that there is always at least a half-brick width between the brick gaps of adjacent courses or layers. If, for example, a particular line of bricks starts from a corner with a full-length brick, the next layer or course above it should start with a half brick.

The cross-sectional size and shape of the chimney will be dictated by the type of clay chimney liner being used. These can be either circular or of square cross-section.

If circular liners are being used, the depth of the brick chimney should be such that the liner just touches the bricks on two sides. The width of the chimney is taken to be that dimension which runs along the line of the wall against which the chimney is being constructed. The depth of the chimney is that dimension which emerges at right angles from the house wall.

The outer chimney construction starts with the building of a profile of bricks on the foundation base of a size that will match the liners being used. This is built up to the level of the hole in the wall through which the flue emerges. The hollow cavity contained by this brick foundation structure is packed with hard rubble and cement.

The flue junction is placed in position on this hard core and the connection with the flue from the fire is made, taking care that the joint is air-tight. A proprietary non-setting sealing compound should be used to make the join. A soot door, available as a standard fitting from most builders' merchants, should be built in at this level.

Now the main construction begins. Because bricks are less heavy units to carry, it may be possible to complete the construction just using a ladder although scaffolding is preferable. Depending upon the type chosen the individual clay liners will be between $1\frac{1}{2}$ and $2\frac{1}{2}$ brick thicknesses in height (some are even higher). So far as is possible, construction should be arranged so that no join between two courses of bricks coincides with the join between two flue liners.

At this stage, the decision must be made whether to opt for just air-gap insulation between the chimney liner and the outer wall of the chimney. If the liners are securely installed with just air gaps and the chimney itself is of solid construction, this is probably adequate for most circumstances. However, a filling of expanded clay pellets or pumice pieces will greatly improve the heat-retaining qualities of the chimney and thereby its air draw and overall efficiency.

As has been stated, circular liners will touch the brick outer wall at two points and should be secured at those points with a mounting of concrete. If square-section flue liners are used, a solid run of cement should be laid from each of its four corners to the matching corners of the chimney pillar.

After every three or four courses of bricks have been laid, the air gaps should be filled with whatever insulation has been chosen.

In just the same way as for block and slab chimneys, the chimney construction should be taken up to the roof or ridge-pole level, breaking the lay of roof slates or tiles as necessary, and then on upwards to the final height, finishing off as before.

At this point there will be no indication as to whether the chimney will require a cowl to solve down-draught problems. However, there is another consideration. Should the wall up which the chimney rises face towards the direction of the prevailing winds, then it may be necessary to protect the chimney top against the inroads of driving rain. With a straight vertical drop, there is a strong possibility that rain will run down inside the chimney and collect at the base. While the chimney is being worked and hot, this is no serious problem for the rain water will evaporate before it has any chance of doing harm. Once the chimney is cold, however, there is every likelihood that it may collect at the base of the chimney, damaging the construction and possibly soaking through to cause ugly damp patches on the inner wall of the house. In such a case it is a worthwhile precaution to protect the chimney top with a cowl. There is a multitude of designs available (see pp 109–13), each designed to solve a particular chimney problem. In this case, however, only the simplest type of cowl need be chosen, and preferably one that does not block the direct rise of the chimney and thereby make chimney sweeping difficult.

Photo 68 The Crooked Chimney pub

Terminals

This is a general term to describe any type of chimney topping or 'termination'. There are about a hundred different designs of chimney-pot or cowl on the UK market, each intended to solve a particular problem. In addition, there are many local variations that are handcrafted by builders from whatever materials are lying conveniently to hand. Before a choice of topping can be made, or even a decision made regarding the necessity for one, it may be useful to restate the function of the chimney top as related to the rest of the stove-heating operation (see p 115).

The chimney is the 'exhaust pipe' of the stove. Just as when a car's exhaust becomes blocked the engine ceases to run, so with a chimney, a blocked flue will completely stop a fire's working. Even a partially blocked chimney considerably reduces a fire's heat output.

When hot fire-gas rises up the chimney flue, provided the passage is well constructed and maintained, its condition can be seen to be stable and well protected. That stability and protection end at the point where it escapes to the outside world. Where a river flows out into the sea, its flow of water has to contend with incoming tides, onshore winds and local currents, all of which can prevent or hinder its escape into the wider ocean. Sea walls are built to protect the outflow from the most vulnerable directions. In the same way terminals are placed around or above the chimney top to protect it from those directions to which it is the most exposed.

There have been many histories written of the evolution and development of the stove into the efficient performer the modern instrument is. No matching work seems to have been published on the matter of chimney-pots. Yet an examination of surviving examples around the world will reveal what a diversity of solutions have been devised over the years to the multitude of often complex chimney-flow problems. A consideration of various fire-gas flow problems, and the chimney-top solutions that have been devised to solve them, will make this apparent.

Basically, all cowls work in the same way. Their individual methods may vary widely, but they all set out to secure the same objective, ie to convert down-draught into up-draught. A selection of modern cowls will indicate the variety of techniques adopted. It is impossible to deliver a blanket judgment as to which cowl is the best buy. Each must be considered on its merits and a decision made as to the most suitable.

The Clark chimney cowl can be fitted to most terminals. Although now out of production, it can still be found in some ironmongers and builders' merchants. It is supplied in three parts with a weatherproof releasable tie to secure the cowl to the chimney top. The cowl consists of a rotatable body covered with a flap. Smoke rising from the fire can escape beneath the flap. A small vane causes the flap body to rotate so that it always faces the wind. Thus, down-draught pressures are prevented from affecting the flue, while the smoke remains free to escape.

The Colt chimney cowl has no moving parts and is easy to install. It consists of a

roughly squared body with curved sides, slotted at each corner. As air flows across these curved sections, the effect is much like that of a plane's wing. The air speeds up and creates what on a wing would be lift, but in this instance, becomes up-draught.

The Aspiromatic is a rotating wind-powered ventilator. Manufactured in France, it consists of a series of curved vanes to form a rotating ball on a low-friction, self-lubricating mounting (see photograph). The ball is hinged so that it can be lifted to one side when the chimney is to be swept. Wind from any direction causes the ball to rotate and this generates up-draft in the chimney.

One of the most interesting designs is the OH down-draught-preventing chimney cowl. This is shaped like a tall 'H. Air can flow into the cowl from any one of four entries, and it makes no difference from which direction the wind comes, nor where it

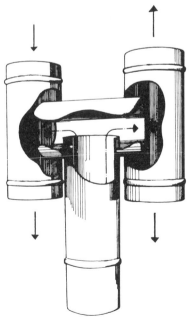

Fig 48 OH cowl

Photo 71 Faral Tropical cowls

Photo 72 Exhausto fan-driven chimney cowl

Photo 70 The chimney museum at Spindleberries,
Tollard Royal, Wiltshire

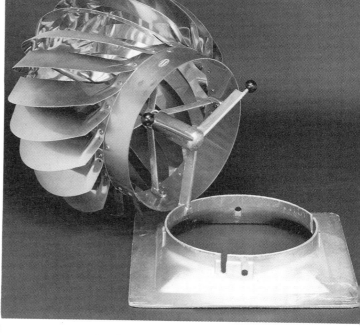

Photos 73 & 74 Aspiromatic rotating cowl

makes its entry. The reason for this is that all moving air must pass along the central, horizontal connecting section. This air exerts a 'pull' on the air in the chimney coming from the fire. This pull is by capillary attraction or friction pull. In other words, the action is similar to that of a scent spray or a car's carburettor. The up-draught velocity produced is about equal to a third of the speed of the wind prevailing at the time. The cowl can be supplied in stainless or galvanised steel, or in red earthenware or buff-coloured fire-clay.

A museum at Spindleberries, Tollard Royal, Wiltshire, houses an exhibition of about a hundred cowls.

Photo 75 The Clark's Chimney Cowl (see p 108)

Photo 76 Fuel Miser Cowl

Photo 77 The Jomoco Special Cowl

Photo 78 Another cowl from the Chimney Museum

114

6 Operational Techniques

Draughts

Before making any judgments as to good or bad performance in heating systems, it is necessary to establish how they work and what constitutes good and bad practice. It is not possible to separate the function of the stove from that of the chimney. They work together as a unit and are the two integrated parts of a whole heat-making engine.

An analogy would be with the engine of a car. The functioning of the carburettor cannot be isolated from that of the petrol pump. A fire needs a regular supply of fuel and air, and so does a car engine. If air does not flow continuously into the cylinders (or the fire-chamber) from the carburettor (or air vents), there will be no ignition and no heat will be generated (all the energy produced by the car engine is, initially, in the form of heat, some of which is translated into propulsion). Once the heat energy has been produced, it can be utilised to create the desired effect – locomotion in the case of the car and house-heating from the domestic fire. In both cases the residual gases must be provided with an escape route, and this also is vital to the working of the entire system. A car engine will stop working if its exhaust is plugged; a stove fire will stop burning if its chimney is blocked.

The car engine's power is controlled by the rise and fall of the air flow (actually air plus fuel) through the carburettor. As the accelerator is pushed down or allowed to rise, a valve opens or closes to regulate the air flow. The stove's heat output is controlled by opening or closing the air vents to increase or decrease the flow of air into the fire. In both cases, the method of energy control will not work if there is any fault in the working of the exhaust system, which means, in the case of a fire, the chimney flue. It is necessary, therefore, to examine in some greater detail the creation of draught in and by this chimney flue.

One of the universal physical laws is that, where movement is possible, less dense substances rise and matter of greater density falls. Most types of wood float in water because, volume for volume, wood weighs less than water. If, however, the wood becomes waterlogged it will just barely float or may even sink. Some very dense tropical woods will not float at all.

Another physical law is that hot substances expand and cold material contracts. If, therefore, you take $1m^3$ ($1.3yd^3$) of air and heat it, the air will expand and occupy a volume greater than a cubic metre so that the original cubic metre now contains less air than before which is, as a consequence, less dense. This warm air, therefore, will rise and continue to rise until its density (ie weight per unit of volume) equals that of the surrounding air.

The amount of expansion in hot substances is in proportion to how hot they are. Very hot material will expand more than less hot material. By the same token, very hot air will rise in a chimney more rapidly than less hot air. From this it can be seen that to retain the heat of the fire-gas within the chimney is important if the fire below is to work at its peak level of efficiency. The more rapidly the flue-gas rises, the more fresh air will be pulled through the fire and the more rapidly will the fire burn and generate more heat.

For the purpose of effective heat-output control, this is the proper way round. The fire must first be worked at the level of peak efficiency, and then its output controlled down to whatever level is required. It is not practical, for the reasons explained above, to work the fire at a level of sub-efficiency and then expect it to rise to peak output simply by control adjustment. It is always easier to work down than to work up.

The importance of retaining a high temperature in the flue-gas is of particular concern in the case of wood burning appliances. At 120°C (248°F) wood tar is precipitated on the inner walls. A further fall in the flue-gas temperature to 90°C (195°F) will result in water condensation. This is not pure water,

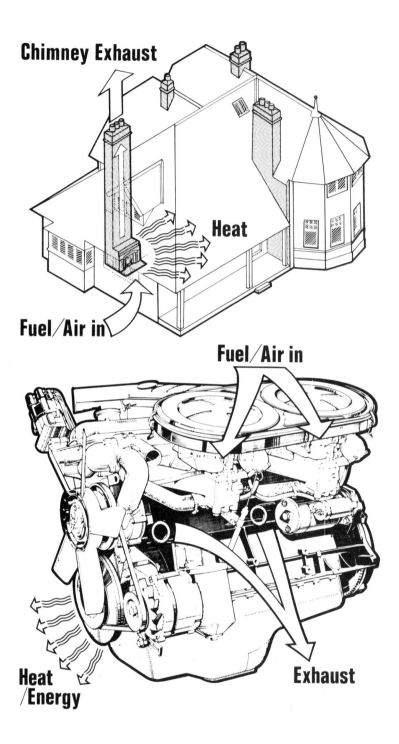

Chimney Exhaust

Heat

Fuel/Air in

Fuel/Air in

Heat/Energy

Exhaust

Fig 49

but a fluid containing corrosive sulphur and other acids. 1kg (2.2lb) of wood can produce 1kg (2.2lb) impure water. 1kg (2.2lb) of coal can deposit $^1/_2$kg (1.1lb) of corrosive fluid at this temperature. Very severe damage can result, particularly in prefabricated metal flues. Poorly designed flues with impaired draught can reduce the working life of a metal flue to as short as five years – in extreme cases, even less.

A proper understanding of the need for good draughting in the working of a fire can eliminate many possible serious problems. Good draught flow results in good fire-burning efficiency. Good chimney design – a good flue shape, the absence of constrictions or bends and effective insulation – will ensure good fire draughting.

As a matter of basic working principle, a straight chimney flue is better than one with bends. Even a single curve in a chimney imposes additional friction between the fire-gas and the chimney wall, slowing it down. Ideally, a chimney should be vertical throughout its entire length. A flue at an angle away from the vertical hinders the fire-gas flow. The gas being hot, seeks to rise vertically, but the inclined flue forces it sideways. This results in additional friction between the gas and the upper surface of the flue producing a reduced speed of flow.

A few figures will demonstrate the importance of chimney condition in the speed with which flue-gas rises up through it. An open fire needs about five times the draught of a closed stove. A solid fuel fire (ie coal burning), either open or closed, needs about twice the draught of any wood-burning equivalent.

An ordinary unlined brick chimney of traditional construction can lose as much as 10°C (18°F) of heat for every metre (3ft 3$^1/_2$in) of height. Suppose there is a good fire burning in a grate or stove. The flue-gas temperature at the base of the chimney will probably be somewhere about 200°C (390°F). If the chimney is 10m (about 32$^1/_2$ft) high, by the time the flue-gas escapes to the exterior at the top, its temperature has fallen to 100°C (212°F). Consequently, its speed of rise is halved and this feeds back and slows down the gas in the lower part of the flue.

It is often suggested that draught problems can be solved by making a chimney taller, but if the condition of the chimney is not good, ie

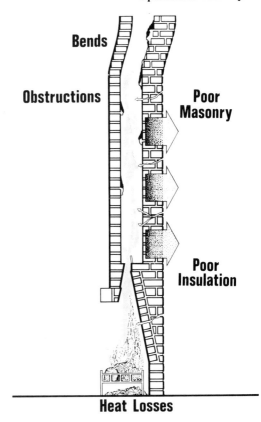

Heat Losses

Fig 50 Heat losses in the chimney

it is not air-tight and well insulated to retain heat throughout its length, a taller chimney could have a disastrously poorer performance than a shorter one.

Poor Draught

If when the fire is lit in the stove or fireplace, it simply flickers with very little energy or heat output and smoke curls lazily up into the chimney and some escapes back into the room, one must first consider whether it is a permanent or a temporary condition. If it is temporary, then the answer is most likely to be found outside the house. If it is permanent, however – if it occurs every time the fire is lit – then the search for a solution must start inside the house.

Internal problems affect open fires more than they do closed, air-tight stoves because the latter consume considerably less air than the former. In fact, an open fire can gobble up as much as 260m³ (340yd³) of air per hour,

117

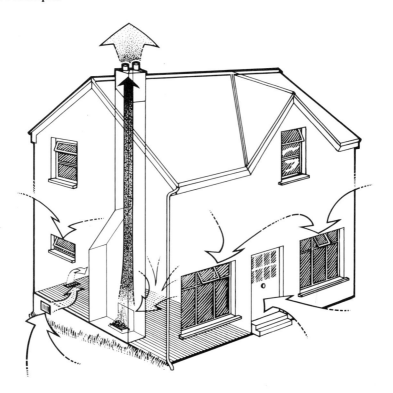

Fig 51 Air flow into the house and up the chimney

which is about ten times as much as that needed by a comparable closed stove (ie about 25m³ (38yd³) of air per hour). This immediately points up the benefit of being able to control to a fine degree the amount of air flowing into a fire.

With this aspect in mind, consider how the air which is surging into the fire to make it burn and then rises up the chimney as hot fire-gas is to be replaced by new air flowing into the room. Since nature abhors a vacuum the air must be replaced. If no air flows into the room, then no air can flow out and the fire will not burn.

If the room in question is double-glazed and protected against draughts, and if it is on the ground floor of a house whose foundation is a solid raft of concrete, then it may be a room which is so close to being hermetically sealed that not enough air can come into it to make the fire work properly.

Make a simple test. With the fire burning, open a window. If the fire picks up almost at once, the problem has been identified as lack of air. Obviously, it is not possible to live with doors and windows open, but draught-proof

vents can be fitted to windows. Alternatively, a ventilation vent can be fitted above a door between two rooms. Air-bricks can be fitted low down in the wall. If the room has a wooden floor, vents can be inserted in the flooring to take in underhouse air.

If the fire does not pick up when the open window test is tried, consider when the chimney was last swept and whether there is evidence of a blockage.

Perhaps the fault occurs with the installation itself. If the problem lies with the air supply into the room, it may be solved by replacing an open fire with a closed stove. However, this is a costly remedy. A compromise may be workable. A throat restricter can be fitted at the base of the chimney flue. While this will not make an open fire as fully efficient as a closed stove, it may halve its air requirement to somewhere about 150m³ (196yd³) per hour.

If the fire still does not burn well and there remains an escape of smoke into the room, one should consider the other possible causes. The fireplace itself could be at fault for grates are often placed in a fireplace whose opening is too high. To test whether this is the case, cut a piece of cardboard wide

118

enough to cover the fireplace opening and deep enough to diminish significantly its opening. With the fire alight, place the cardboard in position across the top of the fireplace opening. If the smoking ceases and the fire burns brighter, the problem has been identified. A permanent canopy or closure plate can be fitted. This, coupled with a throat control, should provide a permanent solution.

Another possibility is that the entire fireplace is too large for the available flue. Consider a domestic funnel – the type used in the kitchen to pour liquids into jars. The funnel has a natural capacity based on the size of its broad end and the dimension of its narrow end. If liquid is poured into it too quickly, the level will build up at the wide end, and if the flow of liquid into the funnel is not reduced there will be an overspill. The same relationship exists between the wide entry into the fire (this includes the entire fireplace surround) and the size of the chimney flue.

Let us consider a fairly wide fireplace, measuring some 600 x 400mm (24 x 16in). To accommodate all the hot fire-gas rising from a fire burning in such a setting will require a flue of not less than 200mm (8in) diameter. If the fitted flue is smaller than this, it will not be able to carry away all the smoke and hot gas generated and there will be a spillage into the room. This problem is often compounded with a flue throat that is too wide and badly shaped.

There is no quick and easy test to determine if this is the problem in any particular fire, but a rule of thumb formula may help. Measure the fireplace opening, ie the entire space inside the fire surround, then calculate the cross-sectional area of the flue. The fireplace opening should be no more than ten times the size of the flue. Indeed, in single-storey houses where there are shorter runs of chimney, this should be reduced to a 6:1 ratio. If this proves to be the problem, there is no easy remedy.

Probably the best recommendation (albeit, a costly one) is to replace the open fire with a closed, air-tight stove. (A small canopy or pelmet may offer a cheaper partial solution.) This will be fitted with a proper range of air-control devices. There will be air vents at the base of the fire-chamber and a butterfly valve on the top of the stove casing in the connection to the base of the flue. With the reduced demand for air of the air-tight stove model and the ability to exercise a firm control of the air flow into the fire and its rate of burn,

Fig 52 Faulty fireplace

there should be no further problems. In any case, air-tight stoves are themselves an antidote to smoking chimneys as there is no way the smoke can leak back into the room. However, it is not enough to choose an air-tight stove just for this reason. One requires efficient burning and heat production and this generally, is what is delivered.

A further possibility to investigate are the fire installations. In a recent example the flue from an open fire inset led into a large empty chamber measuring approximately 600 x 300 x 450mm (24 x 12 x 18in). The householder complained of poor draught and smoke spillage. Once this chamber was exposed the reason became clear. Hot fire-gas rose into this chamber, swirled around and became cooled before finding an exit through the flue which was, in any case, a bare 150mm (6in) in diameter and thereby too narrow. The remedy was to key in a length of flue liner from the top of the inset fire to the base of the flue. This at least improved the draught, even if it restricted the fire's capacity to what a 150mm (6in) flue could dispose of.

The point of this diversion is to highlight what should be happening to the fire-gas at the top of the fire and at the base of the flue. When a given flow of gas (or liquid) is made to pass through a restricted aperture it accelerates. This is known as the 'venturi' effect. The reason why fire-chest and chamber installations have a 'gather' (see p 96) is to restrict temporarily the width of the flue. By so doing, the fire-gas is accelerated (ie by the venturi effect) and this helps to give it a swifter passage up the chimney. If there is a badly shaped throat construction at the base of the flue, with fire-gas escaping into wide open spaces, this too will result in a poor draught, a reluctant fire and smoke spillage into the room.

It is usually possible to test for this problem. A small piece of cardboard or flexible metal sheet can be cut and bent so that it can be wedged across the front or base of the throat. The smoke rising from the fire will eddy and swirl and will not have a visibly smooth flow. If the smoke pattern smooths out when the temporary throat entry is in place, however, then the remedy is to make the installation permanent. It may also be necessary to break into the chimney-breast

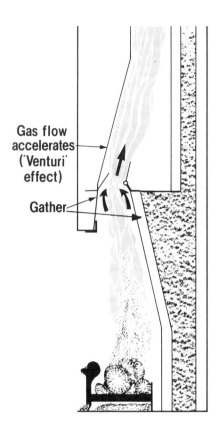

Gas flow accelerates ('Venturi' effect)

Gather

Fig 53 The gather and the venturi effect

and fill in the voids that are ruining the fire-gas flow pattern.

The design of the chimney itself may be a problem, particularly if it is an old chimney for, in the eighteenth century, the curious belief grew up among chimney builders that to create a bend in a chimney flue improved its 'draw'. We know better now, of course, but it is not always easy to put right the mistakes of the past, especially when the angle of bend is more than 45° away from the vertical. In Victorian times it was considered quite normal to bend chimneys almost at whim to make room for other flues or to bypass a fireplace in an upper room. Such bends are often too abrupt, run too near the horizontal for too long and in this twisting mode become too narrow.

Provided a chimney does not suffer all these faults at once, it is possible to improve its performance. If a chimney is sufficiently wide, relining with a modern flue system could be done, ironing out the sharpness of the bends wherever possible. Short sections of the chimney may be rebuilt. The ultimate solution, of course, is to bypass an old chimney completely and build an external chimney flue of some modern design (see pp 95–107).

The possibility of a partial blockage is more common in older chimneys. It sometimes happens that a particular chimney is given the reputation of being a bad chimney and no serious investigation is conducted into causes. A common source of a blockage is very old mortar which dropped down the chimney flue when it was built. It drops as far as a bend, settles there and hardens. Possibly a year later when the chimney is swept for the first time, the flue brush may pass over the mortar, if it is strategically placed on a bend, without dislodging it. Because the brush's rise up the chimney flue is not hindered, no hint is given that such a blockage exists. The test, and often the remedy, is to fit a scraper to the end of the flue-brush rods. Often this is enough not only to reveal the presence of the mortar, but also to remove it.

In a similar way, it is possible for soot to collect in the angle of a bend and become baked hard by the heat of the fire. Again scraping may be the remedy.

In the last resort, it may be necessary to demolish that corner of the chimney flue, remove the blockage manually, and rebuild, perhaps taking the opportunity to insert a smooth lining of some sort so that no anchorage remains for future blockages.

Earlier, the problem of the flue that is too narrow to give passage to the volume of smoke that a fire will produce was examined. The opposite condition, however, may also be a problem. It must be remembered that the proper working of a fireplace and chimney depends on a balance of functions. The fire must produce enough heat to warm the home. It must also throw away enough surplus heat up the chimney to generate sufficient draught to pull in the oxygen that will keep the fire burning. As we have seen already the normal flue diameters in modern stove installations measure 175–225mm (7–9in). Such flues are wide enough to carry away the hot fire-gas and yet narrow enough (with proper insulation) to retain enough heat to keep the fire-gas hot and, thereby, rising rapidly.

Some older houses are found to be fitted with chimney flues more than 305mm (12in) in diameter. Such large flues cause smokiness in a fire because they never get warm enough to impart an active velocity to the rising fire-gas. This meanders up the chimney reducing (by its slowness) the effective capacity of the flue. Surplus gas produced by the fire's burning cannot be carried away by it and spills out into the room. Further, because the fire is burning sluggishly, it produces more smoke in any case.

Fortunately, there is a simple remedy available. Relining with one of the modern systems to the correct dimension will solve this problem. Indeed, it will greatly improve the condition for, no matter what method of relining is adopted, the flue will now have a considerable thickness of insulation around it, consisting of air, liquid cement, rock wool or whatever material is incorporated in the system chosen. Another possible problem arises that is particularly associated with older houses. The difficulty concerns flue liners. Most modern houses that have been built within the last twenty or thirty years

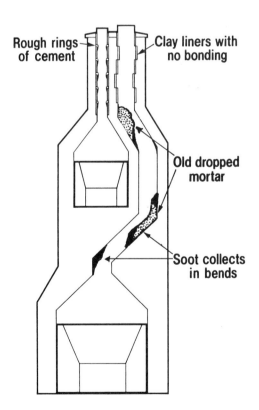

Rough rings of cement

Clay liners with no bonding

Old dropped mortar

Soot collects in bends

Fig 54 Chimney blockage

will probably have chimneys with clay flue liners that fit into each other, ie they have proper joints moulded into them (see pp 103, 107, 131). The terms used are rebated or socketed joints.

Older houses may have flues that consist of clay liners just joined end on to each other (butt jointed). Often these joints are secured with just a rough ring of cement that was never smoothed, leaving a hard ring of cement. A whole chimney lined with such ridges has a built-in obstruction that will considerably slow down the flow of the fire-gas.

Even more serious, in some cases builders simply laid the clay liners end to end against each other without any cement bonding at all. Not only are there likely to be air leaks in such a case, but the liners themselves will fall out of line, creating impedance to the gas flow and cavities where soot or tar can form.

Until recently, the only solution to these problems was, in effect, to totally rebuild the chimney. However, a most ingenious new tool has recently arrived here from Denmark and is available on hire. The operation of the chimney reaming tool is remarkably straight-forward (see pp 175–77). For the present, however, it is restricted to use by trained agents only.

The reaming head is fitted with a grinding chain so as not to transmit shocks laterally into the chimney wall. This is attached to a long flexible drive which is powered by an electric motor. The reaming tool is lowered into the chimney where it is automatically self-centring. It gradually works its way down the ancient and suspect chimney, grinding away all obstructions, cracked clay liners and ridges of concrete. It is adjustable to diameters of between 80mm (3in) and 500mm (20in). At its bottom end, ie the base of the chimney being bored out, there is attached an industrial vacuum cleaner to collect all dust and rubble. The chimney can then be relined with one of the modern stan-dard methods. There is a simple method by which most old chimneys can be inspected to see if they require this treatment. Using a long lead of electrical wire, an ordinary household lightbulb is lowered down the chimney. By its light, from both above and below, the general condition of the chimney liner can be inspected to determine what

degree of refurbishment is called for.

These tests and remedies rise from the base of the installation to the roof-top and beyond, which is where the next possible problem can be discovered. Many builders in the past have been remarkably careless about the chimney-pot terminals they fitted, if any. One of the commonest incompatibilities is the fitting of a round chimney-pot on top of a square-section chimney, which is usually brick built. The result is four awkward obstructing ledges at each of the four corners which, can cause a slowing down of the fire-gas flow. A square-section chimney should always be fitted with a square-based chimney-pot. These are readily obtainable from any reputable builders' merchant.

While the general subject of chimney terminals is dealt with more thoroughly on pp 107 and 122–3, it is worth noting that another aberration of many builders is to fit chimney-pots that taper to a narrow exit in the belief that this will improve the draught and help to keep out wind and rain. It has to be admitted that both these beliefs can have some substance, but they need to be evaluated objectively. Lower down the chimney, just above the fire, there is a very strong tempera-ture differential between the fire-gas in the chimney and the air surrounding it outside the flue. The fire-gas is very hot, the surrounding air is relatively cool. As a result, the fire-gas rises rapidly and at such a velocity that when a narrowing device, such as a flue throat, is placed in its path, it accelerates significantly. By the time the fire-gas reaches the top of the chimney, however, it has cooled considerably and there is no longer the same great temper-ature difference between it and the outside air so that any so-called venturi-tube effect, ie speeding up by passing a flow of gas through a narrowing aperture, is going to be minimal and almost certainly of less effect than external factors such as back-pressure or down-draught.

As to the rain factor, when the fire is burning the up-draught from it will prevent any rain from entering. When it is not working, because rain very seldom falls verti-cally but at an angle, the amount of rain entering is so minimal as to be not worth consideration. Generally, the only rain that gets in will merely dampen the inner surface for a distance of a foot or so. This dries away

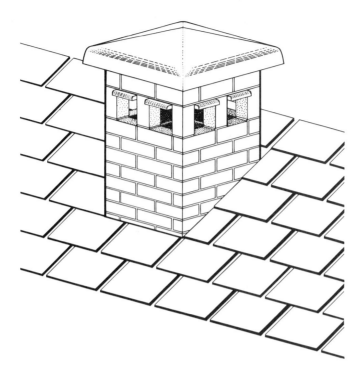

Fig 55 Dove-cot chimney top

when the rain stops or when the fire is next lit. If, for a particular reason, protection against rain is needed, then a cowl especially designed for that function should be installed. In particular, it is important to choose a chimney terminal that is not going to make chimney sweeping difficult or impossible.

If the chimney still does not draw well, check the fuel. In some districts the household coal sold has an above-average tar content. With all the high-and-low-temperature variables of continuous working (especially in winter), this can result in the depositing of combined soot and tar mix that bakes on hard to the inner surface of the liner, especially towards the top where it may also affect the pot or terminal. These flue deposits may become so hard that the sweep's brush will not remove them. Something with the equivalent hardness of a hammer and chisel may be necessary. Where it occurs, removal is the first priority. In districts where the local fuel has this propensity, it is advisable to remove the existing pot and take out any hard-baked deposits lower down in the chimney with long-handled tools. Thereafter, the pot should be replaced with one shorter and wider, and the flaunching (ie the top

finish on the pot or terminal) should be carried up as high as practicable. This replacement pot should have parallel sides with a diameter of not less than 200mm (8in) and a salt-glazed internal lining. If this remedy does not solve the problem, it is possible that a brick-built dove-cot top may solve the difficulty. Failing this, the final measure is to burn nothing but smokeless fuel in that particular grate or stove.

Two installation faults can result in poor draught. These generally are typical of the vast gap that now exists between old and new technology. Where a modern stove is fitted into an old chimney-breast for simplicity, convenience and saving on costs, the installer sometimes simply runs a short length of flue-pipe from the stove fire-chest or chamber up into the large empty void of the old breast. Naturally, hot gases rising from the fire swirl around this space, cooling, before rising up into the flue. Naturally, this kills most of the draught. The remedy is to extend the flue-pipe from the top of the fire and seal it into the base of the chimney so that there is a continuous closed flow of gas.

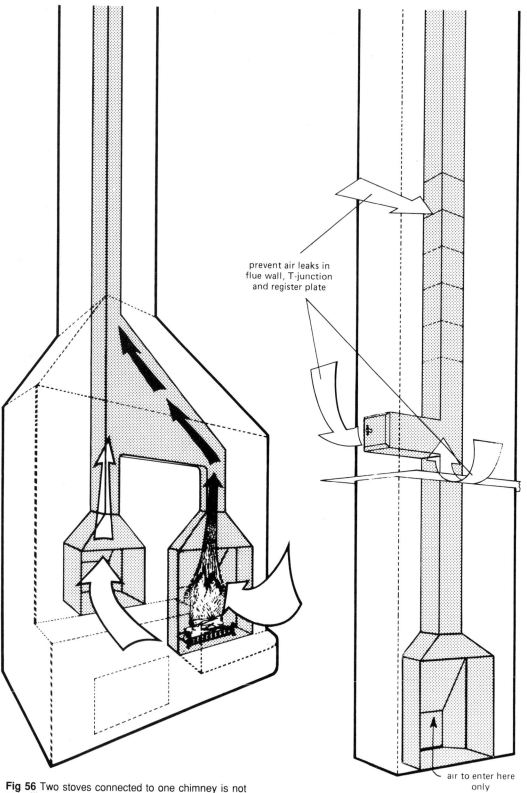

prevent air leaks in
flue wall, T-junction
and register plate

air to enter here
only

Fig 56 Two stoves connected to one chimney is not only illegal and dangerous, but also halves their drawing efficiency

Fig 57 Chimney leaks

Similarly, free-standing stoves that are fitted into an old fireplace with a rear flue-pipe so close to the gather section of the fire-back that there is insufficient capacity to carry away the volume of hot gas produced. The stove can be moved forward or its flue-pipe cut back. If the chimney-breast is too wide at this point, it may be necessary to carry the flue-pipe right up to some level where the original chimney narrows enough to allow the flue-pipe to be sealed into it.

One final cause of poor draught in the chimney is that of air leakage. Any cool air from the exterior that leaks into the chimney flue will cool the fire-gases and cause them to slow down. Apart from the obvious possibilities of leaks in the actual fabric of the chimney, other points that are sometimes overlooked are leaks around the edge of a register plate (ie the plate that seals the base of an old chimney) where it butts against old brickwork, or the surrounding joints in flue-pipes where they pass through register plates and brickwork, or the joints of flue pipes and soot doors. Check also to ensure that in an old house, no air is being drawn into a flue from another fireplace. It was the custom in times past to connect two or more fireplaces to the one chimney. The result is that the draught generated by the fire is pulling in cold air from the other fireplaces and not through the fire that is burning, which consequently dies down. Not only is this arrangement inefficient but, in certain circumstances (as, for example, when back-pressure causes a reverse flow of fumes), there may be a leakage of dangerous fumes into the house.

All accessible joints can be checked by running a lighted taper around their edges. Any leak will show itself by deflecting the taper flame towards itself. Other leaks can be checked by smoke tests (see pp 103, 120 and 131).

Leaks can be sealed with fire-clay, hot-grade varieties of bitumastic sealer, string or tape similarly used. Brickwork leaks can be put right by relining the chimney (see pp 167–8).

No Draught

This is a rare and extreme condition which occurs as a result of long-term neglect in proper and regular chimney-flue maintenance. The condition is manifest usually at the end of a long period during which the fire has not been in use, say, at the end of the summer and autumn. When an attempt is made to light the fire, smoke billows into the room, none apparently being able to escape up the chimney.

There are two most likely causes, both working in combination. If a chimney is not swept and is then used during the winter months, tar and soot can build up in a vulnerable corner of the flue. At the same time the brick structure of the chimney can be attacked by chemical action, resulting in one or more pieces of brick falling down the chimney. These may well lodge at the point where the tar and soot have taken hold, causing a total blockage. Pieces of chimney-pot or slate can also become dislodged and block the chimney.

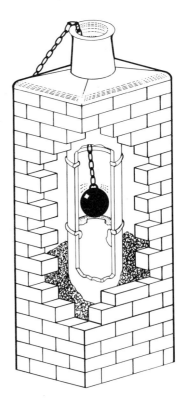

Fig 58 Coring ball

As a matter of urgency, and certainly before any attempt is made to relight the fire, the sweep must be called in. If at the first attempt the sweep's brush will not pass up the chimney, remove the brush and attempt to push the rods alone through the obstruction. If this is unsuccessful, then a coring ball (a heavy metal ball attached to a length of chain) is lowered down the chimney from the roof to remove the obstruction by battering. If even this fails, then a final remedy is to use a chimney reamer (see pp 175–7) to grind away the obstruction. Eventually, that portion of the chimney might have to be cut out and rebuilt.

Once the pieces of brick,slate or pot are dislodged, these will fall to the base of the flue. If the fire is being worked through a narrow gather, some of the pieces might be difficult to work through. To some degree these pieces can be worked through with the fingers from below or, if there is a soot or cleaning door near enough, they can be removed through that opening.

Fig 59 Downdraught on roof, windows and doors

If the flue is connected to a closed stove, this almost certainly will have a butterfly valve fitted into its upper flue connection. Such valves are usually secured by a split pin or nut. Once these are freed, the butterfly valve can be removed and the rubble lowered through.

Down-draught Problems

Down-draught is one of the most pernicious of all chimney problems and seemingly the most difficult for the ordinary householder to come to terms with. Principally, this is because to understand the nature of the problem attention must focus not just simply on the chimney, but on the whole house, and especially the roof.

Let us imagine that the house in question has a ridge-pole running its entire length, with a roof sloping down from it on each side. Just to make the condition more apparent, let it be assumed also that the chimney emerges through one of these slopes and terminates below the ridge pole level. (This should never

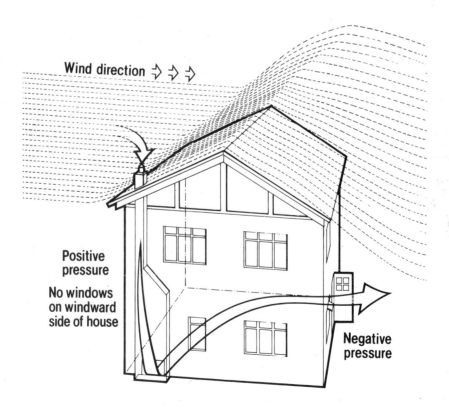

happen in practice; the chimney terminal must be at least 1m (3ft 3½in) above ridge-pole height.) A further assumption is that the side of the house faces the direction from which the prevailing wind comes.

As can be seen from the diagram, when the wind bears against the side of the house, the roof forces it upwards. It flows up over the roof and down the farther side. In this mode it is functioning virtually as a large aircraft wing. Positive air pressure exists on the chimney side of the roof and negative pressure on the lee side. This means that air is being forced into the house on the positive side and sucked out of the house on the down-wind side so that a condition exists in which the air pressure at the top of the chimney is actually higher than that inside the house. Naturally, in these circumstances, pressure is being exerted to force the fire-gas to flow back down the chimney flue, and the fire's heat may not be strong enough to overcome this. In any case, it is likely that the fire-gas flow upwards will be sluggish.

In the terms by which the condition is explained here, this situation will only arise when the wind comes from a particular quarter. For example, should the wind flow be reversed so that the chimney now rises from the roof on the down-wind side, then the negative pressure zone in which it is now placed will accelerate the rate at which the fire-gas rises in the chimney.

The most severe form of down-draught smokiness occurs when there are windows and doors on the down-wind or low-pressure side of the house and none on the up-wind or high-pressure side. A test for the condition can be made if there is any kind of opening (door, window, hatch, etc) on the up-wind side. If this is opened, the pressure inside the house will equalise and the smoky condition should disappear. However, it is not to be contemplated that you would wish to run your fire in cold weather with one or more doors and windows left wide open. Remedies must be found.

As has been suggested, the most immediate remedy is to raise the height of the chimney terminal to a position not less than 1m (3ft 3½in) above ridge-pole height. This should take it out of the high-pressure zone on the up-wind side of the roof. However, in the real world, such a simplistic solution is seldom available. For centuries builders have known better than to terminate chimney tops at below roof height, and for many years building regulations have forbidden it.

When a problem chimney is surrounded by roofs that are taller, or by tall stands of trees, these create much turbulence, the exact pattern of this turbulence being indicated by the direction from which the wind comes. A haphazard system of high-and low-pressure zones is created temporarily, and if the chimney happens to be in one of these high-pressure zones when the wind blows from the direction prevailing in the district, then a smoky chimney will result. (Equally, the wind from another quarter may result in the chimney being in a low-pressure zone which will improve its performance.)

The solution to such a down-draught problem is to equip the chimney top with a cowl. There are at least a hundred different cowls available, each designed to solve a particular problem and it is a matter of patience and fine judgment to determine which is the appropriate model to fit (see pp 107–13 and the section on wind belts pp 9, 26).

There is another set of circumstances that affect the performance of the chimney and yet have nothing directly to do with it. This is a condition sometimes found in single-storey dwellings, or the top-floor flats in apartment blocks. The problem arises from the external shape of the building and its relationship to the wind from one or more particular directions. As the wind flows around the building it creates positive and negative pressure zones – pressure and suction. This can cause air to flow out of a particular room, lowering its pressure relative to the external air. In this condition, fire-gas will be pulled back down into the room rather than escaping up the chimney.

The test for this problem is to generate a volume of smoke in the hearth or stove and watch its movement. If instead of moving towards the chimney it drifts towards either door or windows, then the condition is diagnosed.

This condition is more particularly related to open fires. The easiest and most immediate remedy, therefore, is to install a closed air-tight stove. The more controlled fire-gas flow from this should be strong enough to over-

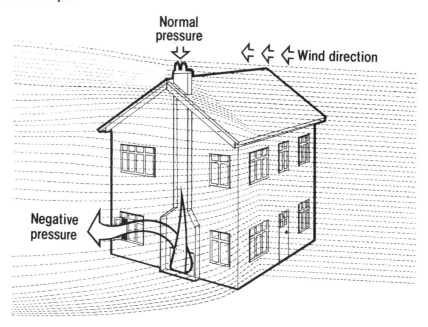

Normal pressure

Wind direction

Negative pressure

Fig 60 Negative internal pressure

come the room's negative pressure. If this alone is not enough, the most powerful form of up-draught cowl, possibly of 'H' form design, should be fitted to the chimney-pot. Additionally, a flue throat restricter at the base of the flue will further reduce the fire-gas flow capacity, increase its retention of heat and, by the venturi effect, accelerate its departure.

Apart from the turbulence factor, down-draught may occur in a chimney from time to time because of another type of relationship with surrounding high buildings. As wind flows towards a chimney top it may have to pass above a taller building. The air swirls downward on the lee side (see illustration) and if this is where the chimney is positioned, a down-draught can be caused that will send smoke billowing back down the flue and into the house. Confirmation of this condition can often be secured by an external check. Smoke will be seen to escape sluggishly from the chimney top and then to flow downwards from it.

Apart from high buildings, this condition in an old building can be caused by nearby stands of tall trees, hillsides or other chimney tops in a stack. If the problem is found in an old stack it can sometimes be solved by capping adjacent unused chimneys which

prevents the syphoning effect. Alternatively, the chimney in question can be heightened a foot or so to raise it above the down-draught level. Otherwise, the remedy is to top the chimney with a suitable cowl that will create an up-draught in the chimney regardless of the external conditions (see pp 108, 112, 127).

Curiously, wind can sometimes have the opposite effect by inducing an excess smoke flow in the chimney to the point where the fire is always burning too strongly and may become difficult to control. In rare cases it may be desirable to fit an adjustable draught stabiliser at the base of the flue. Generally, however, and particularly with air-tight stoves, a combination of bottom vents with a flue butterfly valve is adequate to cope with any condition, even when this may be extreme.

Exposed Flue

Circumstances exist where a flue appears to be physically blocked, although no evidence of blockage can be found. This happens when the upper part of the chimney in the open air is badly sided and made of the wrong materials.

It sometimes occurs that, owing to the particular design of a house, only a short portion of the chimney is inside the house, leaving an exposed tall stack outside. If this is not insulated or protected in any way, and is made of such unsuitable material as cast-iron or asbestos cement, then the fire-gas inside will cool so rapidly that it will cease to rise. Naturally, this prevents any fire-gas movement below. In addition, if the flue damper or fire thermostat has been closed for a long period, the chimney draught may again be reduced to the point where virtually no gas rise can take place.

Apart from the inconvenience of having a fire that will not draw, the condition can be dangerous. If the fire is burning badly, much unburnt gas can escape into the flue. Some of these gases may be dangerously harmful. If the fire-gas does not rise sufficiently to carry these away, they can seep back into the house: young children and the elderly are particularly vulnerable to such fumes.

To diagnose the condition, first check that there is no physical obstruction in the flue. If not, then light a small screw of newspaper in the fireplace or stove and watch the smoke pattern. At first the smoke will curl in almost any direction, but after a minute or so it should begin to rise toward the base of the flue. If this does not happen, it may be necessary to give the chimney a boost. The intention is to generate enough heat to overcome the inertia of the cold air in the upper part of the chimney. To do this, fill the fireplace with a heap of newspaper, each sheet screwed into an individual twist. When lit, these will create a large and rapid blaze which may be enough to get the flue-gas moving. If not, a gas poker or hot-air igniter (even an electric hair-drier) may be powerful enough to have the required effect. (If a gas poker is used, make sure that all its jets are alight, otherwise dangerous unburnt explosive gas can rise and accumulate in the chimney).

It may be that the condition arises because the installed stove is too powerful for the output required of it. For this reason it is worked for long periods at a very slow, damped-down rate. This allows the 'heating table' in the chimney to creep down gradually lower and lower until almost all fire-gas movement ceases. One remedy to this situation would be to give the fire more work to do by installing one or more radiators, a towel rail, or something similar.

Short-term remedies will help to get the fire working again. Long term, the upper reaches of the chimney should be of the proper materials and adequately insulated.

Tar and Soot Damage

The current vogue for slow overnight burning in coal- and wood-burning stoves unwittingly creates the ideal conditions for the formation of tar (in wood-burning stoves) and soot (in coal-burning stoves) on the inner surface of the flue. It is not generally realised that slow burning for long periods (several hours or even days) is something which very few stoves are designed to achieve. In most cases, when a stove is damped down for slow overnight heating, or when it is kept working to that regimen for longer periods, although only a small amount of heat is being generated, this is not, in fact efficient working. Most stoves work very inefficiently when burning slowly and, as a result, a good deal of unburned fuel in the form of gas and vaporised liquid passes up the chimney flue.

The condition of the chimney is more critical for burning wood than it is for solid fuel. Unless it is tinder dry (almost never in ordinary use), wood contains a number of volatile substances. At any temperature below that of full heat (ie when the fire is damped down for overnight burning) a proportion of these remain unburned in the hot fire-gas.

If there is even a minute crack in the chimney wall giving access to the outer air, then, as the fire-gas rises up the flue, it will pull in by capillary attraction or friction, cold air through it. These very small quantities of cold air are enough to lower the temperature of the fire-gas at that point. The unburned volatile components of the fire-gas will precipitate at that level in the form of thick, black, sticky tar (sometimes the tar is more brittle than sticky, but its effect is just the same).

Tar formation poses two difficult problems. In ordinary daily working, tar tends to build up when the fire is set at 'slumber' level. Subsequently, when the air vents are opened up and the heat of the fire is raised (eg in the evenings when the family wish to enjoy the full fire warmth), it is easily possible for the tar in the flue to ignite, creating a chimney

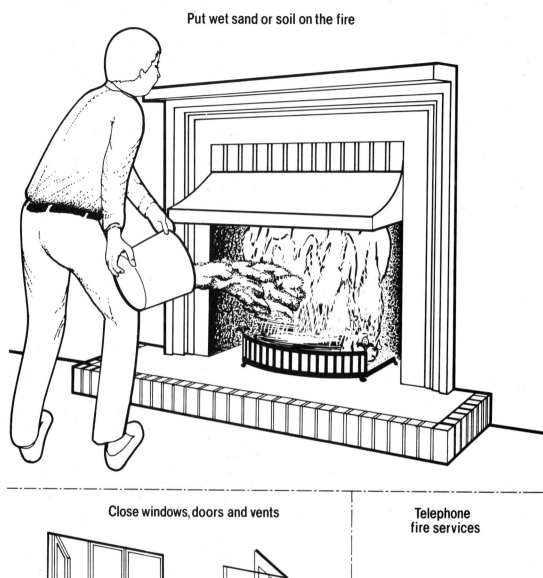

Put wet sand or soil on the fire

Close windows, doors and vents

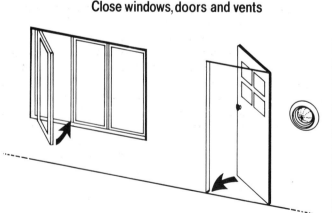

Telephone fire services

Fig 61 Coping with chimney fires

fire of dangerous proportions. Any person who has experienced the full-throated roar of a runaway chimney fire will know what a frightening experience it is.

The remedy is for all air vents to be closed and for the fire to be put out with wet sand or soil from the garden. When you leave the room, make sure that no living-room door or external door is left open. With luck, the chimney fire will burn itself out without doing serious structural damage to the house. An emergency call to the local fire brigade should be made if these precautions do not result in an almost *immediate* reduction in the chimney fire's intensity.

The second problem is longer term and more expensive to correct. With time, the black tar will soak through the porous brick of the chimney and wall. Painted and wallpapered bedroom walls soon become covered with a thick black ooze that continues to spread. The only remedy is to clear and reline the chimney with either multi-skin metal flues or liquid cement (see pp 164–8) and to strip, replaster and decorate the inner walls.

However, it is a simple matter to avoid these circumstances and still preserve the opportunity for slow burning. The fire needs only to be burned hot for some 20–30 minutes each day for any tar or soot deposits to be burned away without the resort to any additional remedy. If the house is equipped with a glass-fronted stove it is easy to keep a watch on this situation. The inner surface of the glass has much the same characteristics as the inner surface of the flue. If the glass remains clear and free of tar or soot deposits, it is a reasonable assumption that the flue is clear also. If, however, there are deposits on the glass, it can be assumed that there will be some deposits on the flue's inner wall. When a daily period of fast or hot burning clears the glass, it almost certainly has cleared the flue at the same time.

It is possible to become much too enthusiastic over the installation of a coal or wood stove and a return to traditional heating, especially when the house in question is an old one with chimneys that, while seeming sound, have not been used for many years.

Before any decision is reached it is important to make a smoke test. Proprietary smoke tablets or powders can be purchased at most stove shops, ironmongers' or builder'

merchants. The procedure is simple and made more simple by modern building regulations that lay down that only one stove or fireplace must be connected to each chimney. If, prior to making the smoke test, it is found that two or more fireplaces (often upstairs and downstairs rooms) feed into the same chimney this is the first item to be remedied.

Ignite the smoke tablet or powder at the base of the flue and place a sheet of metal across the fireplace opening to prevent smoke feeding back. Once a good volume of smoke is generated, follow the line of the chimney upwards, both inside and outside the house, checking at all levels that no wisps of smoke are escaping. Finally, check that there is a strong escape of smoke from the chimney top. Some smoke-test products emit thick clouds of coloured smoke, which is easier to detect.

Once the chimney is filled with smoke it can be useful to close partially the chimney-pot by laying a flat sheet of board or metal across it. This may help to force smoke out through any cracks. The terminal should only be closed for a minute or less, however, as smoke will be forced back into the house through the fireplace.

Experience shows that few old chimneys pass this test without any reservation. At best there is perhaps just a hint in one or more places of a faint escape of smoke. However tempting, and regardless of the pressures generated by the enthusiasm to have a real fire installed and working as quickly as possible, to ignore such signs is a fatal short-cut leading to much inconvenience and additional expense.

The two most immediate remedies are to have the old chimney fully lined by one of the methods described on pp 156 and 101 and the exterior brickwork repointed. Relining with liquid cement or using a flexible double-skin stainless steel liner, may prove to be the most convenient and less costly course, but this is not necessarily so. Each case must be examined on its merits. With long-term prospects in mind, a complete rebuilding of the chimney using the block method or self-supporting ceramic-lined metal flues might be a better answer.

It may be thought that these remedies are too extreme to contemplate. To put them in perspective, however, it is necessary only to consider the alternatives. It is a commonplace among builders specialising in chimney work to be called in when these initial precautions have been ignored and a stove installed anyway.

Wood tar can seep through damaged brickwork into the house and gradually work its way down one or more storeys of inner wall, leaving a disfiguring trail of black and brown patches in its wake. These cannot be painted over. The plaster has to be cut back to the brickwork which must be repointed. The entire wall surface must then be replastered and painted. In addition to this work, the chimney itself must also be repaired, or the condition will return as soon as the fire is put to work.

Deposits of soot can cause corrosive damage to the mortar in the chimney brickwork. Often, the first evidence of this is when hot-spots appear on the inner walls. Eventually, the continuous heat causes these hot-spot patches to darken, cracks appear and smoke begins to escape into the house through them.

Even if the immediate damage is remedied, by cutting away the suspect brickwork through to the flue and replacing it, unless the soot is cleared away and the circumstances that caused it to be deposited in the first place are dealt with and removed, the soot deposits will return and the whole dreary cycle of events be repeated.

Thorough sweeping of the chimney and full relining and repointing are the only solutions, but to follow them through will result in a firm and solid old chimney, possibly in better condition than it was when first built.

Cleaning the Chimney

Although chimney sweeping is a traditional craft, it is governed by strict codes of practice which are administered by the National Association of Chimney Sweeps.

Two provisos stand out as being of concern to the householder. Any person advertising his services by using the name or title of 'sweep' (chimney sweep, etc) is deemed to indicate thereby that he uses the brush method of cleaning and clearing a flue. Any person who uses the term 'vacuum' or 'vac' must clearly indicate if, in addition to the use of such apparatus, he also uses a brush. The brush used must be of an adequate size and strength appropriate to the size of the chimney and the fuel burned in the fire beneath it. The flue brush may be pushed up through the full length of the chimney by rods, or pulled down through it by lines and weights, NACS do not accept that a chimney can be cleaned and cleared by the use of a vacuum cleaner alone. The immediate floor area and fireplace must be sheeted to protect the furnishings from damage and dirt.

Sweeps are exempted from responsibility for damage caused to faulty, aged or damaged chimney-pots, chimneys, flues, heating appliances and cowls.

If, when he arrives at the premises to be swept, a sweep discovers that the situation in which he is being asked to work is unsafe and dangerous, he is entitled to refuse to carry out the work until the defects are remedied (Health and Safety At Work Act (1974)). On producing a written report of the dangerous conditions with suggestions for their remedy, he is entitled to claim his full fee for the work, even though it remains to be done.

To protect their health, sweeps should have with them some form of respiratory protection, fine-weave overalls, protective gloves, a helmet and eye protectors.

When a chimney has been swept, the householder can ask for a certificate to confirm that it has been swept in accordance with the code of practice issued by NACS, as summarised above. This will indicate a suggested date for resweeping. Any obvious defects will also be noted on the certificate.

Any householder who elects to sweep his own chimney is not automatically bound by all the provisions of NACS, although these form a valuable guide. Should there be convenient access to the roof and chimney terminal, it is quite within the ordinary competence of a DIY enthusiast to sweep chimneys satisfactorily, especially in country districts where there is likely to be more room to manoeuvre, and less likelihood of causing disturbance to neighbours.

There is a method that has been used traditionally for many centuries. This requires the use of a small tree, something comparable to the small Christmas tree 1–1$\frac{1}{2}$m (3–4$\frac{1}{2}$ft) in height, together with a length of thin rope long enough to run the full height of the

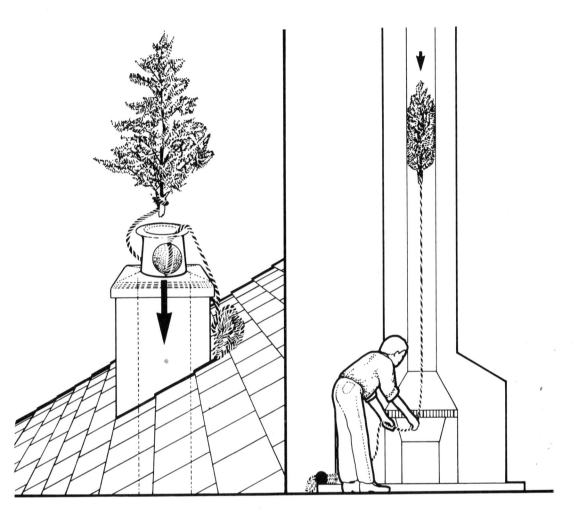

Fig 66 Chimney sweeping

chimney, with some few feet left over with which to work. The rope is firmly tied to the roots or stump of the tree, and to the other end of the rope is tied a large stone or rock of a size that will easily pass through the chimney, including any awkward bends.

The tree with the rope attached is carried up to the roof. There the stone is lowered down through the chimney until it emerges in the fireplace or stove fire-chamber in the room below. The rope is pulled tight and the base of the tree, roots or stump, is firmly inserted in the chimney top. From inside the house, the tree is now pulled slowly but firmly down through the chimney until it has cleared the chimney completely. As it approaches the bottom end, it is useful to have someone with a sack to catch the soot and dust that emerges from the bottom of the flue.

While this may seem a rough-and-ready strategy, it has been used successfully for many years, up to the present day to clear and clean stainless steel and other types of flue. With care it will clear these right down to the bare metal. Used regularly, it will maintain the chimney in good working order.

There are on the market a number of proprietary products that offer a chemical method of cleaning a chimney. These are either in powder or tablet form. Some American offerings are sold as liquids.

To begin treatment, it is generally recommended that the fire be built up to a strong blaze. A measured dose of powder, tablets or liquid is placed on the fire. A chemical gas is released up the chimney and a chemical reaction occurs between this and whatever deposits of soot or tar have formed on the inner lining of the flue. Two possible reactions occur: either the deposits combine with the gas and are burned away, or they liquefy, run down the inner surface of the flue into the fire and are burned there.

Used occasionally, especially to clear persistent deposits, these products are undoubtedly effective. Their original strength has been diminished now so as to lessen the possibility of damage being done to the flue. By the same token, the original 'explosion' that resulted from the combustible character of the products is now almost entirely absent. All that is noticed is a speeding up of the burning rate in the fire when the tablets, powders or liquids are added.

Most of these products emanate from North America where the most usual domestic installation consists of long, unbroken runs of metal-skin flues, mechanically locked together. Wood is the commonest fuel there, although coal is not unknown.

In the UK there has been a sharp reaction against the purely metal-skinned flue. Ceramic liners are more common, both in metal and brick or block chimneys. Sections of flue are relatively short, shorter than is generally the case in North America.

While it is not suggested that there is likely to be any direct damage to the metal or ceramic skin of the flue itself, the possibility exists – the case can be stated no higher than that – that regular use of these chemical remedies, especially if they are used at frequent intervals, might result in the sealing compounds of whatever kind are used to be attacked, deteriorate and become unstable, giving rise to cracks and air penetration. It is suggested, therefore, that such products be used only once a year, just to remove particularly firm deposits, and only as a back-up to the traditional mechanical methods of sweeping. However, if the fire is correctly installed and worked (ie with a 'hot burn' at least once a day), there should be no need for such remedies.

Two useful leaflets are available free of charge from the British Flue and Chimney Manufacturers' Association (see Useful Addresses). They are: *A Guide to Choosing and Using Flues and Chimneys for Domestic Solid Fuel and Woodburning Appliances (including decorative Gas Log and other Fuel Effect Open Fires)* and *A Guide to Flues and Chimneys for Gas Appliances.*

7 Solving the Chimney Problem

There are five main methods of equipping a house with a chimney. They are all equally applicable inside or outside the house.

Brick-built or Slab Chimney with Clay Liner

Although this method is not beyond the ability of a DIY practitioner skilled in brick-building, it is mainly carried out by professional builders in estate development, probably because when building in brick it adds the minimum of cost to use the same technique and material for any chimney. However, it is certainly not the easiest means of producing a chimney that is solidly air-tight and secure against the attack of corrosive substances in the hot fire-gas. To build a chimney that is also totally resistant to the influences of extreme weather conditions demands brickwork of the highest standards.

Equally, keying in the clay liners so that the expansions and contractions of rising and falling flue-gas temperatures do not break the air seal is generally work beyond the competence of the semi-skilled householder.

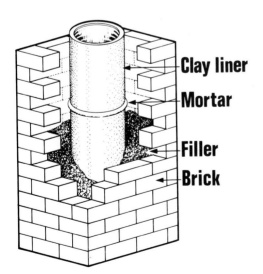

Fig 62 Brick chimney with clay liner

Clay liner

Mortar

Filler

Brick

Block Chimneys

These chimneys are constructed of interlocking blocks made of some type of heat-resistant concrete. (Each block locks into the one below it and the joints in between are made secure with cement.) There are a number of systems distributed nationally and many more that are limited to particular localities. Your local stove shop should be able to advise on what is available. Those selected for inclusion here are marketed throughout the UK and are typical. Each illustrates a specific design or manufacturing theme.

Some manufacturers use the same material to produce both a square section block with an integral flue moulded in the same material, as well as a circular liner suitable for lining existing chimneys. (This method for lining a chimney using flue liners is described on pp 103, 107, 131, 138.)

Insulation is built-in in the form of air gaps or other insulating materials. Chimneys of this kind are relatively simple to erect. They can also be built inside the house, in which case gaps must be cut to allow them to pass through any upper floor and out through the roof. When erected outside the house, a hole for the flue must be made through the base of the outside wall.

Most systems have some type of institutional approval, usually in the form of a certificate from the Board of Agrément, which is issued on the basis of an independent assessment of the system's confirmation to building regulations, manufacturing specification, ease and effectiveness of installation, strength and durability.

Most systems now claim a minimum working life of sixty years, and are guaranteed for fifteen years against damage by chimney fires or corrosion.

The chimney-fire test is probably of the greatest significance to the householder. Despite controlled use of the fire, regular sweeping and maintenance, it is always

135

possible (although unlikely) that some tar or soot may accumulate, often the by-product of extreme circumstances such as acute weather conditions or a sudden fracture in the chimney structure.

A chimney should be able to withstand continuous flue-gas temperatures of at least 600–650°C (1,112°–1,200°F). In the case of a chimney fire, the flue temperature is likely to rise to 1,000–1,200°C (1,830°–2,190°F) which should not damage the chimney. Furthermore, the chimney should not transmit heat. During a chimney fire, its outer surface should not become so hot that surrounding parts of the house may ignite.

Most block systems are claimed to be light in weight. This they undoubtedly are, by comparison with the equivalent volume of bricks. They may still be heavy for some people to carry and what may make them difficult to handle is not so much their weight as bulk. It often needs a long pair of arms to secure a good grip.

However, accepting this, block systems are generally quick and easy to erect and require no skilled labour (see applicable building regulations pp 92, 100, 172). What makes them particularly flexible is that the pumice cement of which they are often constructed can be readily cut by saw, so that liners and casings can be cut to any desired angle (see illustration). Equally, flue connections and soot doors can be fitted at any point.

The central flue can be constructed of the same grade of material as the remainder of the block, or it may feature some type of liner, as in the ceramic block (see pp 89, 105).

Block chimneys are commonly installed with matching fire chambers (see p 141) and some standard design of chimney terminal or cowl.

The Anki Block Chimney System

This is designed and manufactured by Messrs K.E. Kolind & Co (see Useful Addresses) and has been awarded three British Board of Agrément Certificates, Nos 83/1227/8/9. Delivery is available anywhere in the UK, usually within seven days. The company operates a free comprehensive technical service covering all aspects of

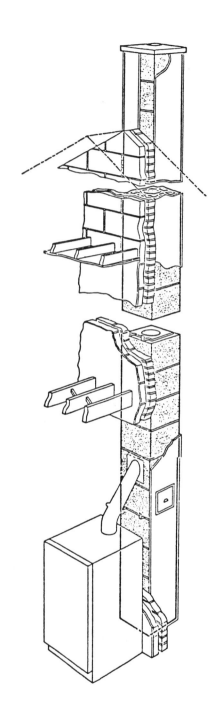

Fig 63 Anki external chimney with square liners

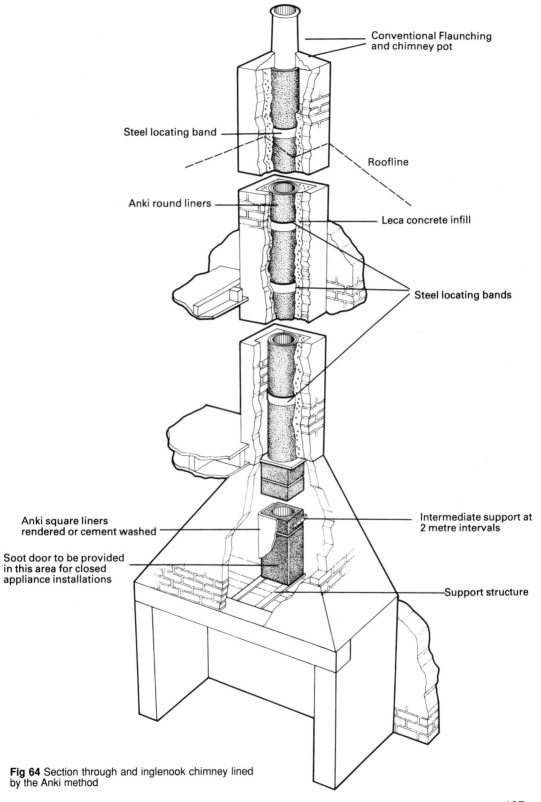

Conventional Flaunching
and chimney pot

Steel locating band

Roofline

Anki round liners

Leca concrete infill

Steel locating bands

Anki square liners
rendered or cement washed

Intermediate support at
2 metre intervals

Soot door to be provided
in this area for closed
appliance installations

Support structure

Fig 64 Section through and inglenook chimney lined
by the Anki method

chimney installation and operational problems (see p 115). The Anki system has been tested and approved for use in Denmark, Sweden, Finland, Germany and the UK.

During the chimney-fire test an internal flue temperature of 1,000°C (1,830°F) was held for 30 minutes. No part of the outer surface of the flue rose above 49°C (120°F). This is roughly the temperature of bath water and is no more than a comfortable handhold heat.

The basic system is of pre-cast units with an integral flue. As a development of this design, there is also a square liner with a round flue. This lacks the air-gap insulation of the complete chimney and is intended to be used where the outer surface is to be brick-clad. There are, additionally, plain round liners to be used for relining existing chimneys (see pp 103, 107, 131).

The individual blocks, which are made of Icelandic pumice bonded with cement (see illustration) are claimed to be lightweight, weighing only a quarter of the equivalent load of bricks. The smallest block weighs 25kg (55lb), but there cannot be too many home owners who would be comfortable humping blocks of that size 390 x 390 x 295mm (15$\frac{1}{2}$ x 15$\frac{1}{2}$ x 11$\frac{3}{4}$in)) weighing a half-hundredweight. The largest block (500 x 500 x 295mm (19$\frac{3}{4}$ x 19$\frac{3}{4}$ x 11$\frac{3}{4}$in)) weighs 36kg (79.2lb).

There are a variety of block shapes available, including one with a built-in cleaning door, an open-sided unit (for easy side-flue connection), one with a corbel to support a brick surround and a capping to complete the top of the chimney stack or terminal.

One problem that may occur somewhat urgently is the lack of provision of any means to bend the flue around curves in the complete chimney system. This seems only to be available in the plain liners with an uninsulated connection between the two systems.

The Isokern Chimney System

This block chimney system is manufactured in Denmark and imported to this country by Kedddy Ltd. It has been awarded British Board of Agrément Certificates Nos 81/865 and 82/1018. It meets International Standard

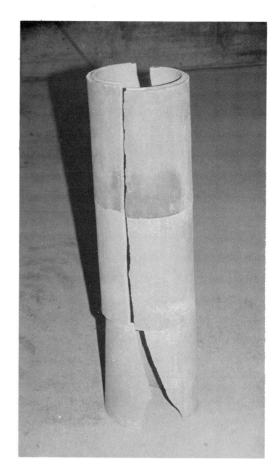

Photo 79 The effect of thermal shock – temperatures of above 1000°C – on a clay liner

ISO 4736 and the Canadian ULC S 629 M. These approvals indicate, among other matters, that the chimney system is suitable for all fuels, including wood and straw, has a working life of at least sixty years (although it is only guaranteed for ten years), can be erected by unskilled labour, withstands continuous fire-gas temperatures of 650°C (1,200°F) and will contain chimney-fire temperatures of 1,200°C (2,190°F) for up to 30 minutes.

The Isokern DM (double module) all fuel chimney system can be used for both single and double flues (although these must be totally separate. The blocks have both square and rectangular cross-sections (see illustration p 139) Both of these have socket and spigot joints for easy and gas-tight assembly. A small gap between the inner and outer surfaces allows for thermal movement

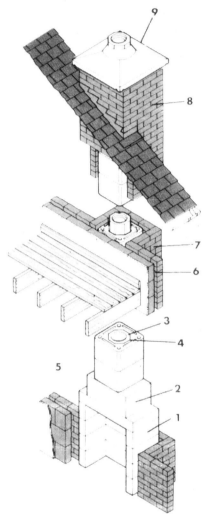

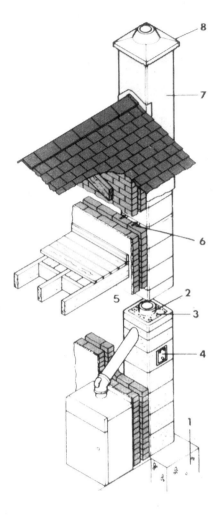

1 Firechest installed so that chimney breast does not intrude on room space.

2 Gather/lintel unit (or 5).

3 Socket and spigot inner flue block.

4 Air and expansion gap between inner flue blocks and outer casings.

5 Lintel provides support for facing bricks or rendered blockwork above fireplace opening (not shown).

6 Conventional cavity provides sufficient clearance from combustible materials in constructing floor.

7 Chimney clad in facing bricks or rendered blockwork.

8 Corbel supporting brick chimney cladding (not shown).

9 Capping to brickwork chimney stack.

1 Concrete foundation.

2 Inner liners.

3 Cavity between outer casings and inner liners fill.

4 Access blocks and soot door providing access to flue.

5 Steel collars to positively locate joints between inner liners (not shown).

6 Stainless-steel wall ties or galvanised-steel straps at 2m intervals tying chimney to building structure.

7 Rendered outer casting.

8 Capping to rendered chimney stack.

Fig 65 Isokern DM external chimney with hole-in-the-wall fireplace

Fig 66 Isokern Standard external chimney

Solving the Chimney Problem

1 Firechest.

2 Socket and spigot inner flue blocks.

3 Air and expansion gap between inner flue blocks and outer casings.

4 Casing should be finished to individual requirements with paint, plaster, render, panelling etc.

5 Corbel supporting brick chimney cladding.

6 Outer casing can be omitted where chimney is to be clad in brick.

7 Capping to brickwork chimney stack.

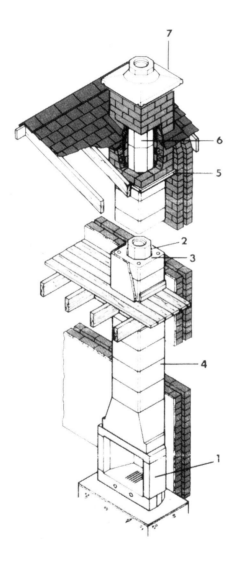

Fig 67 Isokern DM internal chimney

Opposite: **Fig 68** Chimney blocks

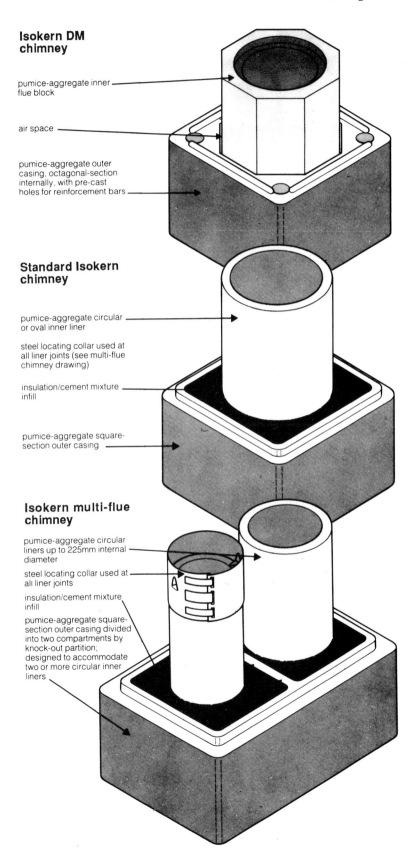

Isokern DM chimney

pumice-aggregate inner flue block

air space

pumice-aggregate outer casing, octagonal-section internally, with pre-cast holes for reinforcement bars

Standard Isokern chimney

pumice-aggregate circular or oval inner liner

steel locating collar used at all liner joints (see multi-flue chimney drawing)

insulation/cement mixture infill

pumice-aggregate square-section outer casing

Isokern multi-flue chimney

pumice-aggregate circular liners up to 225mm internal diameter

steel locating collar used at all liner joints

insulation/cement mixture infill

pumice-aggregate square-section outer casing divided into two compartments by knock-out partition; designed to accommodate two or more circular inner liners

▲ A

▼ B

▲ C

Photos 80–2 (a) Kedddy Isokern block chimney rising through the roof rafters; (b) There are staggered joints between casings and flue blocks; (c) Relining an old chimney with Isokern flue liners

(expansion and contraction), and this removes any possibility of cracking. It also provides insulation. When a chimney extends more than 1.1m (3ft 7in) above the roof, reinforcement bars can be inserted in pre-cast holes in the outer casing.

The outer blocks are 300mm ($11^3/_4$in) high. The inner liners are 650mm ($25^1/_2$in) in length so that, for strength, the joints between the outer blocks and those between the inner liners seldom coincide. The inner liners are secured by steel collars.

Because there is no physical connection between the inner and outer components, any heat expansion of the liners cannot be transmitted to the outer blocks and there is, consequently, no danger of heat-induced cracking.

As the inner and outer sections are not connected, they do not necessarily need to be used together. Ordinary brickwork or any type of building blocks can be used for the outer casing. In such a case Isokern liners with pumice insulation in-filling can be used independently.

Despite the separation between the inner and outer sections, there remains a problem that is a common feature of all block chimney systems, and that is weight. These pieces are heavy and bulky. The smallest size of outer case weighs 22kg (48.4lb). A typical inner liner weighs between 7 and 10kg (15.4 and 22lb). Few householders can comfortably clamber up and down ladders hoisting bulky components of this size.

Isokern block chimneys can be built free-standing (ie not needing any additional support) to a height of 9m (29ft 5$^1/_4$in) with suitable internal reinforcement. Otherwise, chimneys need to be tied in to the wall at 2m (6ft 6 $^1/_2$in) intervals. There is further difficulty with block systems in that they seldom incorporate bend sections. Whenever it is necessary to take the chimney past an obstruction, this can only be achieved by cutting the liners at an appropriate angle with a masonry saw or disc cutter. Isokern will supply purpose-made liner bends, but the external blocks must still be cut to fit. It is not easy for a person with average skills to do this and sustain air-tight joints.

A number of matching accessories, such as cappings, corbels (supports), soot doors, etc., are available.

Photo 83 Kedddy Smokex Chimney fan

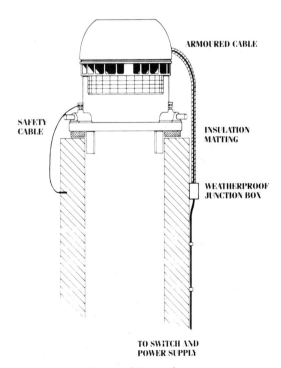

ARMOURED CABLE

SAFETY CABLE

INSULATION MATTING

WEATHERPROOF JUNCTION BOX

TO SWITCH AND POWER SUPPLY

Fig 69 Kedddy Smokex Chimney fan

143

The Kedddy Smokex Chimney Fan

Some degree of controversy surrounds the use of chimney cowls – and in particular, powered fans. Some argue that these serve only to mitigate the symptoms (poor draught, etc.) and do nothing to attack the cause. It has to be accepted that chimney problems are often very complex, and related in a complicated way to the fabric of the building where they occur. Rather than initiate an extremely costly and elaborate rebuilding programme, just to cure a badly performing chimney, it is sometimes a simpler expedient to secure an adequate working, uprising draught in the flue by fitting an electric powered fan – of which the Kedddy Smokex Chimney Fan is an excellent example.

Constructa

One of the simpler and more flexible block chimney systems is made and marketed under the name 'Constructa' by Taylor & Portway Ltd. The entire system is manufactured to the tolerances required by British Standards 2028, 1364, (1968) and is protected by Patent No 1604386. The main blocks, made of Leca aggregate, have a dry weight of 24kg (53lb), causing a weight problem, The block dimensions are proportionate to brick sizes so that they can be keyed into inner or outer walls, including brick or timber party walls, replacing exact numbers of bricks. The separate flue liner, made to British Standard 1181, has a square section that matches that of the main block. Because the liner is deeper than the block, it is rare for outer and inner joints to correspond.

The system includes a choice of fire-openings, chambers and chests, all of which can be put together like a child's building-block set, from the variety of standard block shapes available. All components are designed to be load-bearing, and insulation is by air gap between the inner flue liner and the outer block wall. The illustrations show typical open- and closed- fire installations.

A special wall-flue forming kit is available for building exterior stacks. Thereafter, internal and external construction methods are very similar. Even offset flues can be built with no great difficulty.

Thermoflue

A block chimney system that has been in production for over thirty years. Thermoflue originates in Denmark and is sold in the UK by The Thermoflue Company. The company offers a free advisory service. On application, a questionnaire will be sent on which the exact nature of the chimney installation problem can be diagramised. An emergency 'red line' telephone advisory service is also maintained.

The system holds approvals from a wide variety of national and international institutions and authorities. Dantest, the Danish State Testing Laboratory, conducted the original acceptance tests over thirty years ago and continues to monitor production every three months. It is currently used by developers on many building sites because of its ease of construction – six hours is quoted for the time to erect a 6m (19ft 7½in) chimney, starting from a constructional hearth.

This may be read as a recommendation, but there are reservations. Because of its simplicity of construction and the fact that its base components (fire-chest, etc) are stressed to carry a load of 6 tonnes, some builders install these chimneys directly on the house foundation raft, using this as if it were a constructional hearth. The two should never be amalgamated in this way as, over a period of years, the weight can induce a folding collapse in the raft. This can be confirmed and identified by the appearance of a certain waviness along the ridge-pole a year or so after building.

A Thermoflue chimney must be built on a constructional hearth, mounted on a firm raft that goes down to some stable foundation, ideally well below soil level. However, this caveat should not be taken as a detraction from the qualities of the Thermoflue system itself, which has been awarded the British Board of Agrément Certificate No 84/1422.

Thermoflue also complies with British Standard 6461 (paragraphs 5 and 6). According to the current British Gas Board Approval List No 7, Thermoflue is the only Class I chimney block approved for use with gas appliances, in many cases (so long as the correct flue size is used) without the need for a liner.

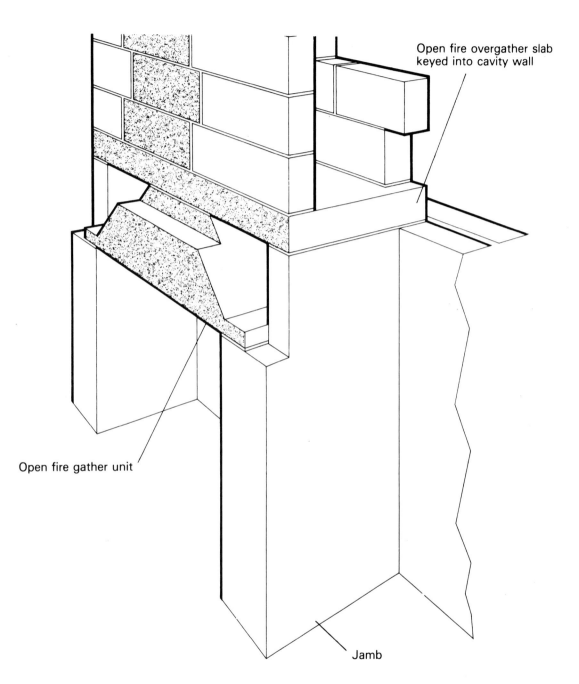

Open fire overgather slab keyed into cavity wall

Open fire gather unit

Jamb

Fig 70 Constructa open fire installation

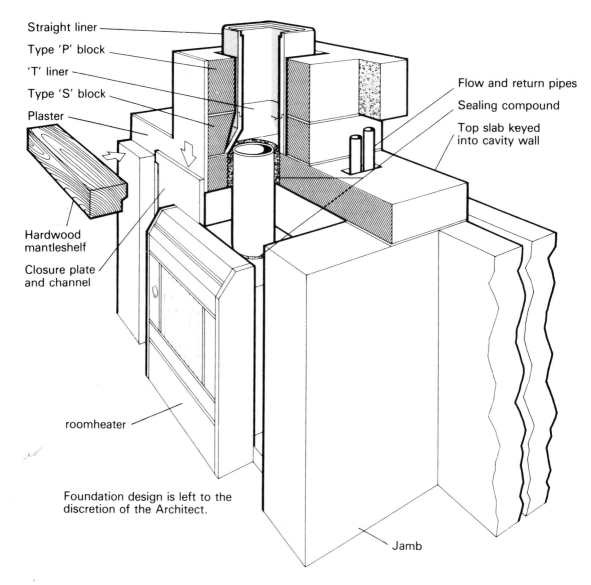

Straight liner

Type 'P' block

'T' liner

Type 'S' block

Plaster

Flow and return pipes

Sealing compound

Top slab keyed into cavity wall

Hardwood mantleshelf

Closure plate and channel

roomheater

Foundation design is left to the discretion of the Architect.

Jamb

Fig 71 Constructa roomheater installation

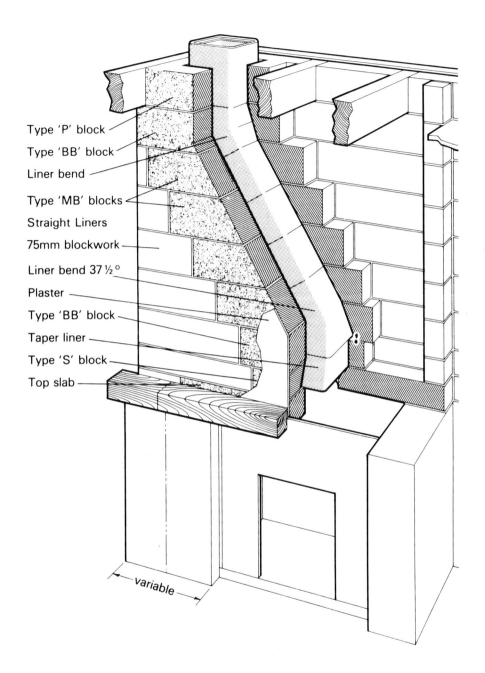

Type 'P' block

Type 'BB' block

Liner bend

Type 'MB' blocks

Straight Liners

75mm blockwork

Liner bend 37½°

Plaster

Type 'BB' block

Taper liner

Type 'S' block

Top slab

variable

Fig 72 Constructa offset chimney construction

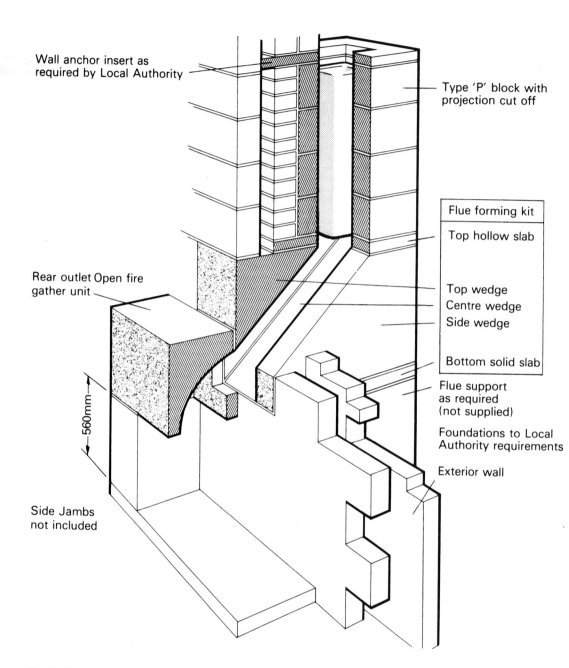

Wall anchor insert as
required by Local Authority

Type 'P' block with
projection cut off

Flue forming kit

Top hollow slab

Rear outlet Open fire
gather unit

Top wedge
Centre wedge
Side wedge

Bottom solid slab

560mm

Flue support
as required
(not supplied)

Foundations to Local
Authority requirements

Exterior wall

Side Jambs
not included

Fig 73 Constructa external chimney construction

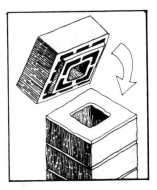

Fig 74 Thermoflue chimney block construction

1. Lay thick mortar bed on recessed closed end facing up.

2. Lay next block on mortar bed with spigot facing down and closed end uppermost.

Fig 75 Thermoflue block chimney passing alongside timber

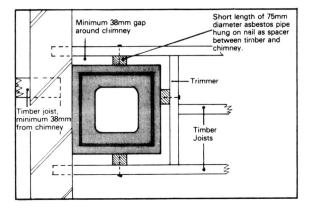

Photo 84 Thermoflue standard chimney block showing the triple-wall construction

149

Solving the Chimney Problem

Fig 76 Thermoflue internal fireplace

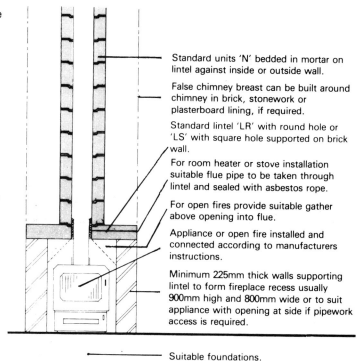

Standard units 'N' bedded in mortar on lintel against inside or outside wall.

False chimney breast can be built around chimney in brick, stonework or plasterboard lining, if required.

Standard lintel 'LR' with round hole or 'LS' with square hole supported on brick wall.

For room heater or stove installation suitable flue pipe to be taken through lintel and sealed with asbestos rope.

For open fires provide suitable gather above opening into flue.

Appliance or open fire installed and connected according to manufacturers instructions.

Minimum 225mm thick walls supporting lintel to form fireplace recess usually 900mm high and 800mm wide or to suit appliance with opening at side if pipework access is required.

Suitable foundations.

Fig 77 Thermoflue chimney and boiler

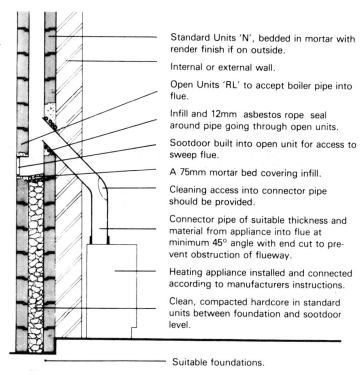

Standard Units 'N', bedded in mortar with render finish if on outside.

Internal or external wall.

Open Units 'RL' to accept boiler pipe into flue.

Infill and 12mm asbestos rope seal around pipe going through open units.

Sootdoor built into open unit for access to sweep flue.

A 75mm mortar bed covering infill.

Cleaning access into connector pipe should be provided.

Connector pipe of suitable thickness and material from appliance into flue at minimum 45° angle with end cut to prevent obstruction of flueway.

Heating appliance installed and connected according to manufacturers instructions.

Clean, compacted hardcore in standard units between foundation and sootdoor level.

Suitable foundations.

150

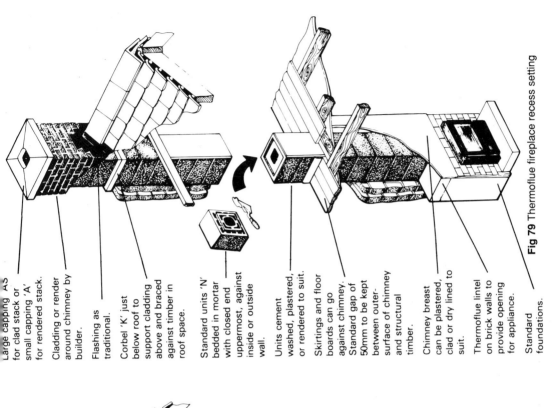

Fig 79 Thermoflue fireplace recess setting

Large capping 'AS' for clad stack or small capping 'A' for rendered stack.

Cladding or render around chimney by builder.

Flashing as traditional.

Corbel 'K' just below roof to support cladding above and braced against timber in roof space.

Standard units 'N' bedded in mortar with closed end uppermost, against inside or outside wall.

Units cement washed, plastered, or rendered to suit.

Skirtings and floor boards can go against chimney. Standard gap of 50mm to be kept between outer-surface of chimney and structural timber.

Chimney breast can be plastered, clad or dry lined to suit.

Thermoflue lintel on brick walls to provide opening for appliance.

Standard foundations.

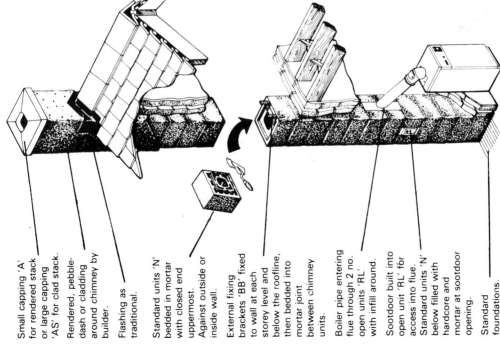

Fig 78 Thermoflue external boiler chimney

Small capping 'A' for rendered stack or large capping 'AS' for clad stack.

Rendered, pebble-dash or cladding around chimney by builder.

Flashing as traditional.

Standard units 'N' bedded in mortar with closed end uppermost. Against outside or inside wall.

External fixing brackets 'BB' fixed to wall at each storey level and below the roofline, then bedded into mortar joint between chimney units.

Boiler pipe entering flue through 2 no. open units 'RL' with infill around.

Sootdoor built into open unit 'RL' for access into flue. Standard units 'N' below filled with hardcore and mortar at sootdoor opening.

Standard foundations.

151

There is no need here to give detailed descriptions of the various types of installation as the drawings adequately illustrate them:

1 A typical internal fireplace
2 A typical external boiler chimney
3 A fireplace recess setting
4 A boiler-type setting

The installation of chimneys in both timber-frame and masonry-wall houses is also shown.

Completing these details are illustrations of the Thermogather (which makes the connection between the base of the flue and the upper level of the Thermochest), the Thermochest itself, and the means for building offset chimneys.

The Selkirk System

One of the more recent chimney systems to be introduced (the market launch was in May 1985) is the Selkirk block chimney with ceramic liner. It is manufactured and marketed by the Selkirk Division of Household Manufacturing Ltd, an International American Corporation based in Chicago.

The ceramic element is the product of three years intensive development and is composed of mullite-cordierite ceramic. This is incorporated in a square section glass-reinforced concrete outer shell with a lightweight, highly insulated concrete core (see illustration). Each block stands 225mm (9in) high, equalling three courses of conventional brick, or one course of standard building block, and weighs 24kg (52.8lb).

The heart of the system is the ceramic liner which is designed to withstand continuous flue temperatures of 760°C (1,400°F) and has survived thermal shock tests (ie very rapid temperature rises from cold) up to 1,100°C (2,012°F). The liner is ultimately capable of

Photo 85 Selkirk chimney stack

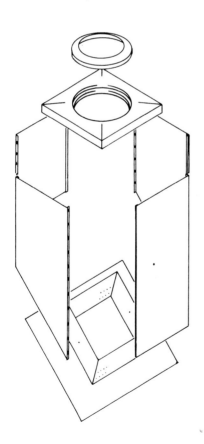

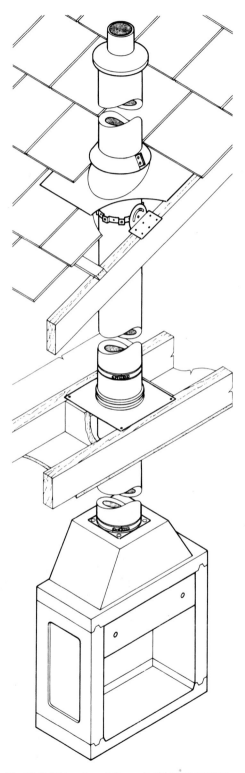

Fig 80 Selkirk external Ceramic chimney system

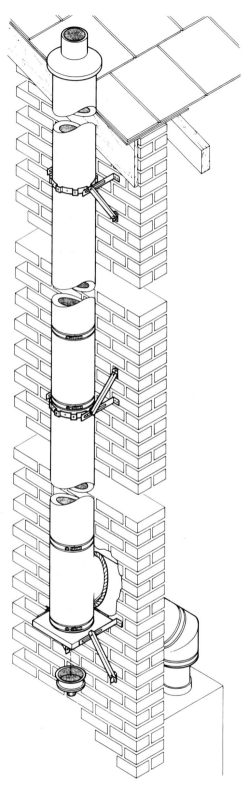

Fig 81 Selkirk internal Ceramic chimney system

Fig 82 Chimney brick cladding

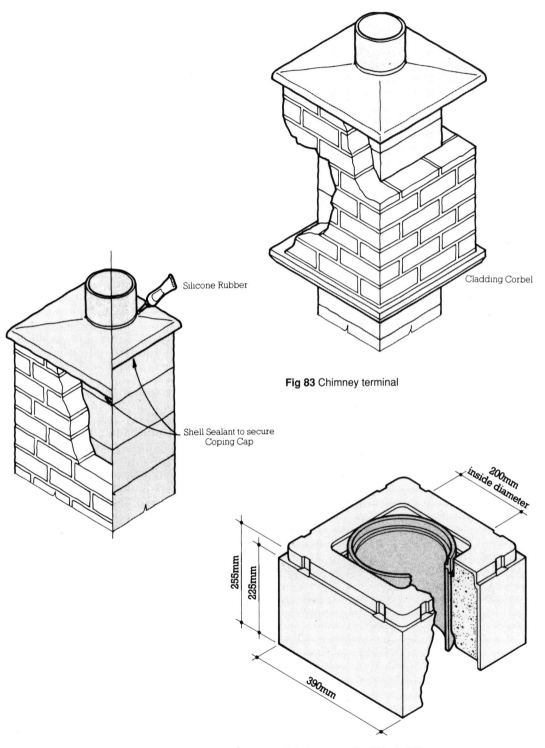

Silicone Rubber

Cladding Corbel

Shell Sealant to secure
Coping Cap

Fig 83 Chimney terminal

200mm
inside diameter

255mm

225mm

390mm

Fig 84 Standard chimney block with ceramic liner

Weight per standard block: 24kg
Weight per metre run: 106kg

155

resisting temperatures of 1,280°C (2,340°F) without distortion or damage.

No British Standard relevant to this chimney system currently exists, but it complies with British Standard 6461, Part I (1984) as regards general construction and composition of materials. A British Board of Agrément Certificate has been applied for. Meanwhile, the liner exceeds the requirements of the German DIN Standards 18147 and 18150. It also satisfies the strength, heat and acid-resisting requirements of British Standard 1181. The system is guaranteed for the life of the building in which it is installed.

The blocks are manufactured in accordance with the Pilkington GRC system which utilises specially spun fibre-glass chopped into short lengths and mixed into the concrete. Precision electronic sensoring and metering of all ingredients control the quality of each block. Additionally, specially developed cements are supplied in skeleton-gun cartridges for sealing and bonding the shell to shell, and liner to liner, joints. Both blocks and liners have spigot and socket locks. The outer shell is water-shedding.

The relatively low external temperature of the block surfaces under normal operating conditions allows a chimney of this type to be installed with an air gap of only 38mm (1½ in) separation from any combustible materials, as specified by building regulations.

The maximum vertical run of chimney is 20m (65ft 5in), and the chimney must be secured at every fourth block joint into the wall, using one of three types of wall tie available. Offset and support units are available to allow the chimney to be carried around bends. Each chimney must be topped with either a cladding coping, block coping or pot terminal.

Brief experience with the chimney suggests that it is a relatively easy one for the DIY householder to handle. Certainly, on the grounds of weight alone, the stainless steel system is preferable to the block chimney. It weighs 46.2lb per metre run in the 125mm (5in) size.

Prefabricated Chimneys

These come in two forms: metal and refrac-tory. As with block chimneys, these also come in standard sections that interlock. While block chimneys are generally self-supporting, prefabricated chimneys will probably require some supporting ties into the wall, floor or roof at stipulated intervals. Again, such chimneys can be connected to matching fire-chests or chambers.

Steel prefabricated chimneys are insulated in the same way. Double-skin designs use air as an insulating agent or the gap between the two metal skins is filled with some insulating material, such as rock wool.

Systems made of refractory material are similarly packed with insulating material.

Rite-Vent

An interesting comparison between refractory concrete-lined and prefabricated insulated chimneys can be made between the products of one manufacturer: Rite-Vent. The former is marketed under the name Parkaflue, the latter uses the name Parkabest. Both conform to British Standard 4543. In addition, the Parkabest complies with British Standard 1449, Part 2, 1983, in the use of high-grade austenitic stainless steel in its manufacture. The Parkabest was also the first prefabricated chimney to secure the approval of the Danish Ministry of Housing – Approval No G-787/755-93-73. Both utilise the same arrangement of continuous insulation with no internal metal cross-ties through which heat might leach away to the exterior.

The Parkabest patented insulation system consists of moulded mineral wool which is immune to attack by insects or rodents (although how these would gain access to it is not clear) and will not support the growth of fungi or moulds. Both chimneys have been tested to temperatures of 1,100°C (2,012°F).

Erection times of 2–3 hours are quoted for both systems, neither of which requires the use of special tools, and no wet working is involved. Different locking methods are used. The Parkaflue employs spigots and sockets while the Parkabest is secured by locking bands.

However, a detailed examination of the two structures, from the inner linings

Photo 86 Selkirk Ceramic twin-wall insulated chimney

157

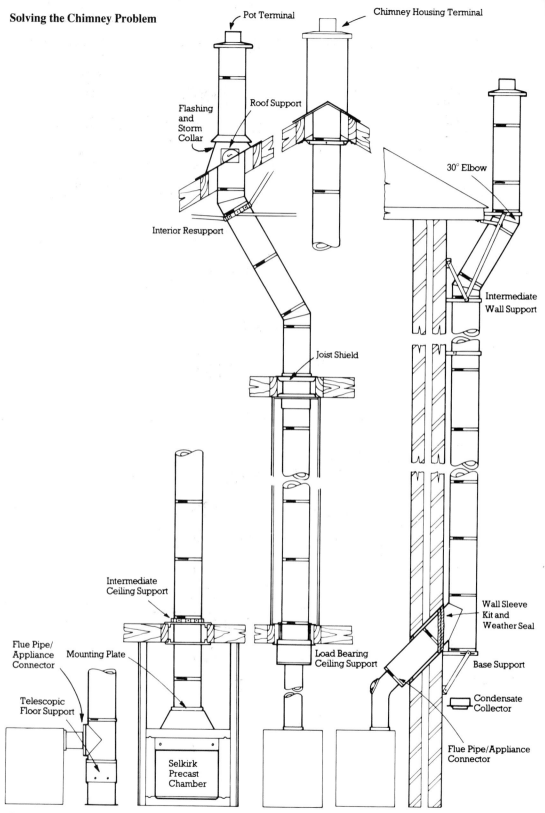

Fig 86 Selkirk Ceramic chimney – typical applications

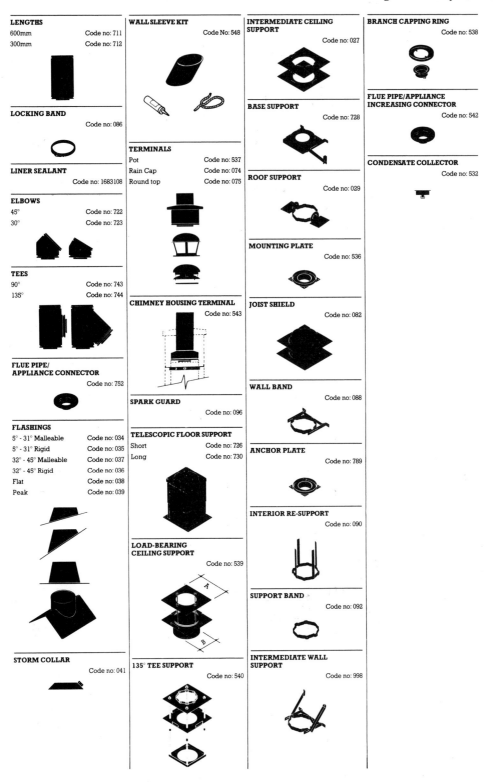

LENGTHS
600mm   Code no: 711
300mm   Code no: 712

LOCKING BAND
               Code no: 086

LINER SEALANT
               Code no: 1683108

ELBOWS
45°   Code no: 722
30°   Code no: 723

TEES
90°   Code no: 743
135°   Code no: 744

**FLUE PIPE/
APPLIANCE CONNECTOR**
               Code no: 752

FLASHINGS
5° - 31° Malleable   Code no: 034
5° - 31° Rigid   Code no: 035
32° - 45° Malleable Code no: 037
32° - 45° Rigid   Code no: 036
Flat   Code no: 038
Peak   Code no: 039

STORM COLLAR
               Code no: 041

WALL SLEEVE KIT   Code No: 548

TERMINALS
Pot   Code no: 537
Rain Cap   Code no: 074
Round top   Code no: 075

CHIMNEY HOUSING TERMINAL
               Code no: 543

SPARK GUARD
               Code no: 096

TELESCOPIC FLOOR SUPPORT
Short   Code no: 726
Long   Code no: 730

**LOAD-BEARING
CEILING SUPPORT**
               Code no: 539

135° TEE SUPPORT
               Code no: 540

**INTERMEDIATE CEILING
SUPPORT**
               Code no: 027

BASE SUPPORT
               Code no: 728

ROOF SUPPORT
               Code no: 029

MOUNTING PLATE
               Code no: 536

JOIST SHIELD
               Code no: 082

WALL BAND
               Code no: 088

ANCHOR PLATE
               Code no: 789

INTERIOR RE-SUPPORT
               Code no: 090

SUPPORT BAND
               Code no: 092

**INTERMEDIATE WALL
SUPPORT**
               Code no: 998

BRANCH CAPPING RING
               Code no: 538

**FLUE PIPE/APPLIANCE
INCREASING CONNECTOR**
               Code no: 542

CONDENSATE COLLECTOR
               Code no: 532

Fig 87 Selkirk Ceramic chimney components

159

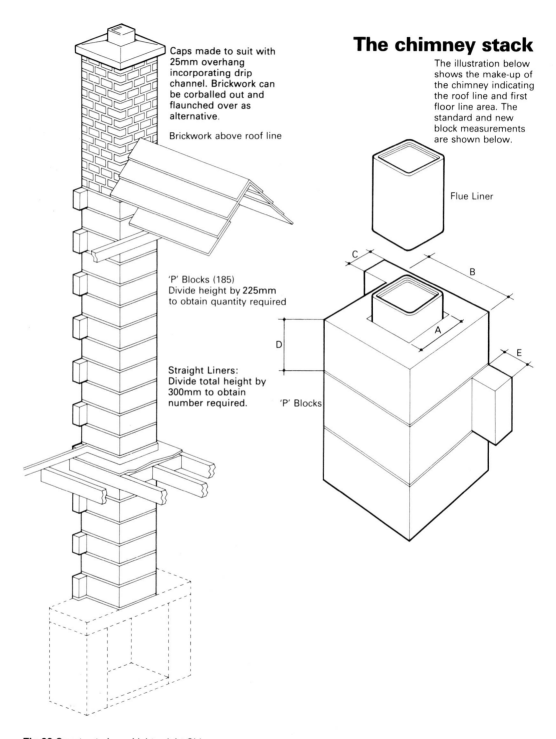

Caps made to suit with 25mm overhang incorporating drip channel. Brickwork can be corballed out and flaunched over as alternative.

Brickwork above roof line

'P' Blocks (185)
Divide height by 225mm
to obtain quantity required

Straight Liners:
Divide total height by 300mm to obtain number required.

'P' Blocks

The chimney stack

The illustration below shows the make-up of the chimney indicating the roof line and first floor line area. The standard and new block measurements are shown below.

Flue Liner

C

B

D

A

E

Fig 88 Constructa Leca Lightweight Chimneys

160

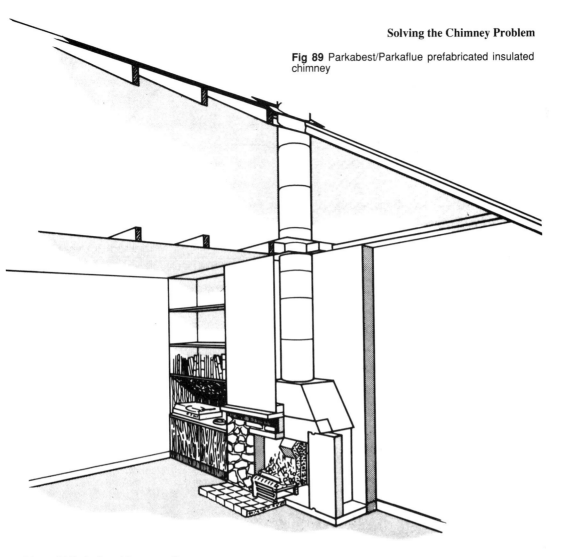

Fig 89 Parkabest/Parkaflue prefabricated insulated chimney

Photo 87 Parkaflue chimney sections

161

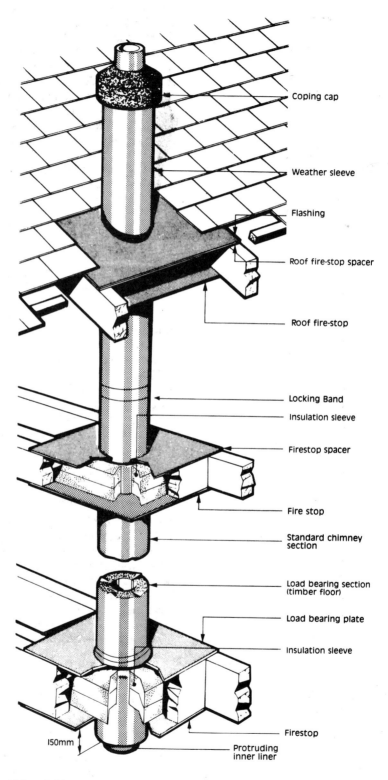

Coping cap

Weather sleeve

Flashing

Roof fire-stop spacer

Roof fire-stop

Locking Band

Insulation sleeve

Firestop spacer

Fire stop

Standard chimney section

Load bearing section (timber floor)

Load bearing plate

Insulation sleeve

150mm

Firestop

Protruding inner liner

Fig 90 Parkabest internal chimney

162

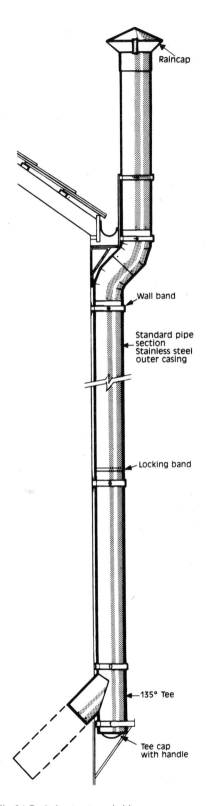

Raincap

Wall band

Standard pipe section
Stainless steel outer casing

Locking band

135° Tee

Tee cap with handle

Fig 91 Parkabest external chimney

outwards, discloses important distinctions. The Parkabest has a stainless steel inner lining, backed by the moulded insulation already described. The whole is contained within an outer casing of galvanised steel (finished in electrostatically coated grey epoxy resin paint) or stainless steel.

Distinctly different, the Parkaflue incorporates a unique, dense refractory concrete liner which, at high temperatures, fuses to form a ceramic bond. The same moulded insulation is fitted, as in the Parkabest. Similar outer casings are utilised – galvanised steel for internal use, stainless steel for exterior construction. The Parkaflue spigot and socket lock is contoured so that any precipitated condensates run down the inner wall of the chimney into the fire and are burned. The Parkaflue has been granted British Board of Agrément Certificate No 84/1259.

Two important factors emerge from this comparison. The Parkaflue is undoubtedly the more durable and longer lasting installation. It is also heavier and somewhat more difficult to erect to satisfactory standards, and is more costly. The Parkabest proves to be more vulnerable to stainless steel destabilisation, yet is lighter and easier to erect. Typical internal and external installations are illustrated.

Flexible Metal Chimneys

These are relatively new to the UK market and not yet time-tested, although they have performed satisfactorily elsewhere.

Single-skin flexible chimney liners have been available in Britain for many years. These have been considered unsuited to solid-fuel or wood-burning use, particularly because of their lack of air-tightness and poor insulation. They are restricted by building regulations to use with gas-burning appliances only.

New double-skin designs are now available with strong recommendations from other countries, notably Canada and France. The inner surface of the flexible flue is smooth in one direction, (so it is important during installation to ensure the liner is used the right way up) and bends of up to 90° can be made of fairly small radius. Such a system

163

can be used to line an existing chimney, or it can stand alone as a chimney flue with suitable wall supports.

Flexible Double-skin Liners

It may be that the existing chimney in a house is in a relatively poor condition, and yet not bad enough to pull down and reconstruct. If there are bends in its run of no more than 45° away from the vertical, then one way of bringing its overall condition up to one where a first-class draw can be expected is to reline it with a double-skin stainless steel flexible flue. Although experience of such chimney liners has been very limited in this country, they have been in use for several years in France where the French Board of Agrément (CSTB) have awarded it a certificate of approval (Technical Assessment No 11/83-134).

The method of installation is remarkably simple, and work that in most other types of chimney lining would take several hours to complete, can with luck and care by this method be completed in under a minute. Ideally, two people should make the installation.

It is necessary for the interior installation of the stove to which the flue liner is to be connected to be completed and the stove firmly mounted in its permanent position. The existing chimney must be checked to see that there are no obstructions to the free run of the flexible flue.

A length of flexible flue is not particularly heavy and well within the capacity of one person to lift and carry. Using a ladder one person climbs up to the roof stack through which the flue is to be inserted, carrying one end of the flue length. It is important to make sure that the end raised to the roof for insertion down the existing chimney is that end which, in the final installation, is to be at the bottom of the run. An examination of the inner surface of the flexible flue will make clear why this is necessary. Viewed from one end the inner surface will be seen to be composed of a series of small ridges. The presence of these ridges can be confirmed by running the fingers up and down the inner surface. It is possible for the flue-gas to impinge upon these ridges with the possible layering of tar and soot.

However, from the opposite direction, a visual inspection and confirmation from the fingers will make clear that the run of the surface is smooth, and it is this section that must be mounted at the bottom of the chimney so that the flue-gas has a smooth rise upwards.

This established, the first person climbs to the roof carrying the full length of flexible liner. This is inserted vertically downwards in the chimney top. The person remaining on the ground feeds the back end or remainder of the flue up to the roof, climbing up the ladder to deliver the tail end. The person inserting the flue into the chimney top must make sure that the first section to be inserted is straight, or as near straight as can be managed. Thereafter, the flue needs only to be pushed down the chimney until its bottom end reaches the flue connection on the top of the stove below. It is made firm with a connecting sleeve and sealed with fire-clay or sealing compound.

Any remaining section of flexible flue extending above the chimney top can be easily removed with a metal saw. Care should be taken when doing this as the folds in the metal forming the flexible double skin tend to come apart when cut. This exposes jagged edges on which the fingers can be badly cut. The top of the chimney can now be finished off normally (see pp 123, 166).

At least two days should be allowed for the chimney sealants to become completely dry before lighting a fire in the stove.

Multiflex

For the house with a suspect chimney, new options are becoming available. Relining with refractory concrete is one; reaming and relining is another. A third involves the use of flexible, double-skin metal flue-liners made of high-grade stainless steel. In some ways, these are the easiest of all liners to install. (The photographs show a typical one-man installation, completed in less than one day without expert assistance.)

Photos 86–91 Installing the Multiflex chimney liner. (a) lowering Multiflex into chimney; (b) guiding Multiflex into chimney; (c) sealing the connector onto the gather; (d) securing the bottom support brackets; *(see overleaf)*

▲ A

▲ C

▼ B

▼ D

Photo 92(e) Installing the Multiflex chimney, continued: fitting the register plate

Photo 93(f) Fitting the chimney pot over the Multiflex terminal

In the late Seventies, single-skin flexible metal flue-liners were briefly on sale in the UK. For most people, experience of these was disastrous. Under flexion the flues did not retain their air-tightness. Their insulating qualities were, as a consequence, poor, resulting in the rapid build-up of wood tar and coal soot. These induced fairly rapid corrosion to the point where the metal flue broke down.

Much has since changed with the introduction of the French Lis'flex double-skin flexible metal flue-liner, made by Société Westaflex of Roubaix and marketed in the UK by Multiflex International Ltd.

While no British Standards exist for flue liners of this type, the Lis'flex has been tested and approved by the Centre Scientifique et Technique du Bâtiment, Paris, from whom it holds Certificate No11/83-134 (the CSTB is the French member of the European Union of Agrément).

Both inner and outer walls are made of austenitic stainless steel, the inner being half as thick again as the outer. The method of manufacture by which the liners are rolled and seamed in a continuous process, ie a continuous spiral wound double, has the effect that while the inner surface is smooth in one direction, it has a ribbed profile in the other. It is important, therefore, that the flue is installed the correct way up so that the flue gas meets only the smooth surface, and not the ribbed.

Bends of up to 45° can be easily accommodated by this flue with little loss of performance in the standard temperature performance tests.

Chimflex

Another flexible, double-skin, stainless steel chimney liner which is available on the UK

166

Photo 94 Coils of Chimflex stainless steel double-skin chimney liner

market, 'Chimflex' comes from France where it has been awarded the CSTB approval certificate No 11/82-132. It is marketed by Rite-Vent Ltd.

In construction, installation and performance, it is virtually identical with Multiflex. It carries the same ten-year guarantee and works to the same temperatures: 250°C (480°F) for continuous burning, up to 500°C (930°F) for fast burning, 750°C (1,380°F) during short critical periods and up to 1,000°C (1,830°F) in an emergency, such as a chimney fire.

Relining with Refractory Cement – Cast *in situ*

This is strictly a professional technique and is not available to the ordinary householder. It is included here for general guidance and so that there can be some reasonable understanding of the methods in progress.

Generally, relining an existing chimney by this method is most appropriate when the chimney is of a reasonably sound structure but requires much detailed attention as to pointing and the replacement of some damaged brickwork. In particular, the type of damage that can be best remedied by this method is that associated with air draughts in the chimney wall that hinder a good draw.

Different practitioners adopt a different sequence for the various essential procedures and this is of no particular significance. Essentially, a long, narrow balloon-like former of reinforced rubberised canvas or plastic is lowered down the entire length of the chimney from roof-top height down to hearth level. This acts as the mould for the chimney run that is to be created or constructed. So that an even thickness of chimney wall is preserved throughout its entire length, spacers are inserted at each bend to hold the balloon away from the existing wall. This means that there will be a certain amount of structural work inside the house. This is necessary because, if the

167

Photo 95 Lining a chimney with liquid cement

chimney-liner wall is of uneven thickness, weak spots will occur wherever the wall is thinner. Not only will this make the chimney structurally suspect at those points, but equally, heat from the fire-gas will leak away to the exterior at those points making them vulnerable to tar or soot formation.

With the chimney prepared to receive it the former is lowered down through the chimney, with care taken at each floor level that it passes smoothly by each spacer without any twist. Once in place, the former is sealed at the bottom end with a metal clamp.

The supply of refractory cement is connected to a small motored pump which raises it to chimney-top height. From here it is poured at a slow, even pace down into the space between the former and the chimney wall. The cement is fairly liquid and sinks down the chimney length without any hindrance. This pumping operation usually takes about a day and must be completed in one single operation.

Many operators take the precaution of securing a weather forecast for the district in which they will be pouring the liquid cement. Obviously, it is desirable to avoid conditions of continuous heavy rain and high wind. Extreme heat or dryness will also affect the drying rate of the chimney cement. If it dries too rapidly, cracks may occur. Chimney lining by this method should never be undertaken when the external temperature is below freezing as this too can affect its ultimate physical stability.

As relining a chimney using refractory cement is a matter of some technical complexity – and it is important to get the procedure right – a professional governing body has been set up by the industry. It is the National Association of Chimney Lining Engineers. NACLE holds a British Board of Agrément Certificate No84/1394 for its recommended chimney lining system, and all its approved installers must work in accord with this system.

Prior to relining, all chimneys must be subjected to an inspection that is itemised under twenty-four headings. Where the structural condition of the chimney is suspect it may be considered necessary to call in a chartered engineer experienced in masonry design to check the stability of the chimney

and to specify any remedial work that may be essential before relining starts. Work of less importance may be recommended by the contractor. This could include rebuilding the stack above the roof line, brick repointing and clearing blockages in the old chimney.

The NACLE check-list is as follows:

1 The age of the property
2 Material used in its construction
3 General condition
4 Evidence of recent structural changes
5 Condition of the exterior
6 Porosity of the mortar and masonry
7 Condition of rendering
8 Condition of chimney stack
9 Movement of internal joists
10 Evidence of internal and external cracks
11 Soundness of sailing courses (ie where there is an overlay between several layers of bricks)
12 Soundness of chimney-pot
13 Evidence of masonry falling into the fireplace
14 Condition of chimney-breast
15 Evidence of the escape of flue-gas
16 Facing direction of the flue (ie north, south, east or west)
17 Evidence of building settlement
18 Angle of stack away from the vertical
19 Evidence of widths (ie internal dimensions) collapse
20 Has the flue been reduced by stack rebuilding?
21 Have pot liners been used?
22 Is the site of the soot door acceptable?
23 Is there timber built into the brickwork?
24 Is the chimney suitable for lining?

These checks having been completed, the chimney must then be properly swept. This is followed by a smoke test, in accordance with British Standards Code of Practice 131, 1974. Any serious gas leaks in the chimney revealed by this test must be put right before relining commences. This may involve repointing or replacing faulty brickwork.

The size of the existing flue is of vital importance. It must be wide enough to accommodate the required flue size, plus a minimum thickness of 19mm (³/₄in) of lining concrete. The correct size of balloon is then passed through the chimney, either from the top down, or from the bottom up, through the full height of the chimney. Temporary access openings must be made in the chimney-breast at off-sets or bends, and at intervals not greater than 2m (6ft 7in) in straight sections. This is so that the balloon can be placed in a central position within the flue and held there by formers, thus making sure that the minimum thickness of chimney-liner wall is obtained throughout the length of the chimney run.

With most two-storey house installations where the chimney height is not excessive, the liquid cement is poured down the flue from roof-top level. However, where the chimney height is too great for this to be possible, the cement is poured into the flue through temporary openings made in the chimney wall within the house. Usually the pipe is taken in through the most convenient window, allowing the minimum of disturbance to the house interior.

An important precaution must be taken with this method. The cement is poured right up to the level of the opening through which it is entering the flue. The cement pipe is withdrawn and the opening completely sealed and made air-tight with brick or whatever type of construction is appropriate to the house structure. As soon as the closure is made, the pipe can then be lifted to the next level at which it is planned to pour cement. The point of this arrangement is to make sure that the lower level of cement does not dry out before the next level above it (which is still in liquid state) is poured down on it. Should this happen, there might be some doubt as to the firmness of the bond between the two layers. For this reason, ie to ensure the stability of the concrete liner, the delivery pipe must be lowered down through the chimney top to the lowest level inside the house at which the lining is to start. As the liquid cement is poured, the pipe is slowly raised to remain just above it as the level rises, and so in a continuous operation right to the top. When the wall thickness is excessive, and large volumes are being pumped, at no time must the interval between the top level of the cement in the chimney and the

pipe from which it is being poured be allowed to exceed 2m (6ft 7in). This is so that the various rough bonding agents in the cement mix do not separate out and become unevenly distributed.

Despite all these apparent complexities, the method is a relatively simple one and many house installations are completed in one day. However, a minimum period of twenty-four hours must be allowed for the cement to set hard enough to allow the balloon to be deflated and removed, so the householder must contain himself with a certain patience. Ultimately, it will be to his advantage to see that these procedures are not rushed through. Indeed, in wet weather conditions or during periods of cold (although not at temperatures below freezing), it may be necessary to delay the removal of the balloon by as much as 24 hours from the end of pouring.

Once the balloon is removed, NACLE requires its members to make another smoke test to see that there are no air leaks in the new liner. A check must also be made that the liner exceeds the minimum thickness along its length. All access points are checked, and the chimney-pot is replaced and sealed. Another 48 hours must be allowed to pass before a fire is lit in the grate or stove, and for the first forty-eight hours this fire must be kept at a low level

This technique of chimney lining has been available in the UK for about the last ten or twelve years. Experience has indicated that, properly executed, this method supplies an effective and long-lasting installation. Short-cuts, however, are disastrous, and doorstep bargain offers from cowboy operators should be avoided.

The method is of especial value in older buildings where chimneys follow tortuous paths and need structural reinforcement. With old flues, the minimum wall thickness of the liquid liner can be generously exceeded with advantage.

Flue-pipes

The Brefco VE Pipe System

The situation often arises that when a new

Photo 96 An assortment of Brefco Superflue sizes and shapes

Photo 97 Proheat stainless steel flue sections

stove or other heating unit is being newly installed in the house, a connection must be made from it to an existing chimney flue. This needs to be done in the cheapest, simplest and most unobtrusive manner and without disturbing or reducing the performance of the installation that already exists.

Traditionally, cast-iron flue sections would have been used, but cast-iron is now an expensive material and remains brittle and easily damaged by knocking. It is heavy and awkward to work with since it cannot be bent or cut. A modern answer is to use cheaper (approximately a third to a half of the price of cast iron), lighter and more malleable stainless steel pipes. These, however, have not in themselves proved to be as resistant to corrosion and acid attack as was first anticipated. This deficiency is now made up by the use of vitreous enamel which is not merely painted on, but fused into the metal at a temperature of 840°C (1,550°F).

In the case of the Brefco System, two coats of vitreous enamel are applied in this way to both the outer and inner surfaces. Black, white and brown are standard finishes. These flues are designed for interior use up to a maximum length of 1.8m (6ft) and are joined by spigot and socket. A variety of units are supplied ranging from straight sections (with cleaning door if required), bends, tees, elbows and cowls.

Installations of this type are now covered by new building regulations that prohibit a horizontal flue connection from a stove into a flue or chimney of a greater length than 150mm (6in).

The Proheat SS Flue System

This single-wall stainless steel flue system is manufactured by Prowoda Heat Ltd. Two types are available: SS 316 for gas/oil/solid fuel appliances, and the SS 430, in effect, for industrial use.

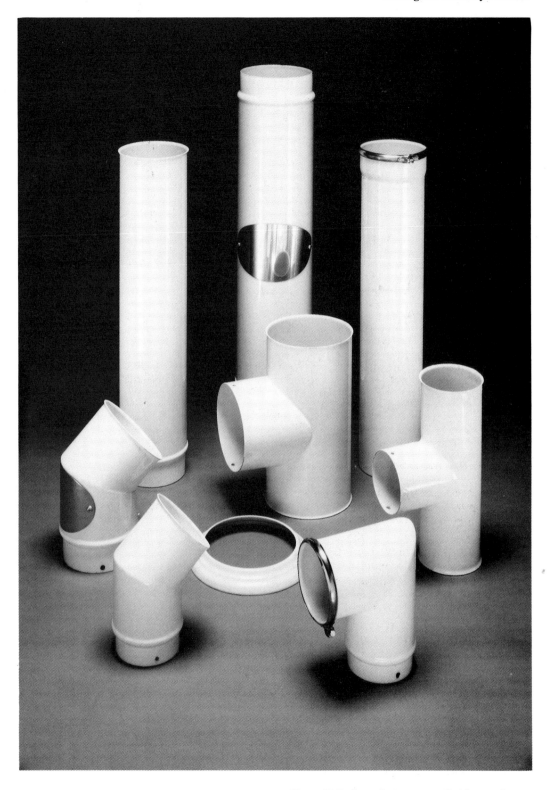

Photo 98 Proheat vitreous enamelled flue sections

173

Photo 99 Externit asbestos compound flue sections

174

This system has a precise and somewhat limited domestic application, namely, it is intended to line an existing chimney rather than to be used as a complete chimney system in its own right.

Used as a chimney liner, it would utilise the air gap remaining between itself and the chimney-flue inner wall as an insulating gap.

As such, it represents a halfway house between a traditional chimney (perhaps of somewhat doubtful condition) and a fully insulated, double-skin modern flue system. This may be tenable in certain circumstances, eg where an existing chimney is in a reasonably sound condition apart from some small air leaks that would prevent the efficient use of a modern appliance, where a lining of this type may create a workable and reliable flue (see photograph).

Proheat Vitreous Enamelled Flues

This flue system, also manufactured in the UK by Prowoda Heat Ltd, utilises a conventional spigot and socket connection between sections, with a quick locking joint clamp closed by a screw. Intended for DIY use, it conforms to British Standard 6441, Part 2, 1984. Its enamel covering conforms to British Standard 1344, Parts 1, 3 and 7. General comments concerning the validity of vitreous enamel flues have already been made (p173).

The most interesting and original feature of the assembly is a telescopic pipe section that allows the flue length to be altered without any pipe cutting (ie the telescopic section is inserted and slid up or down to fit into any required dimension).

This telescopic pipe has a second important use, in that the chimney can be swept through the COD (clean-out doors). However, should this prove to be unduly awkward, the entire flue system can be removed completely by unscrewing the joint clamp band on the telescopic pipe, and sliding the pipe down.

The sealing compound at the boiler connection then needs to be removed so that the entire flue system can be removed – a drastic remedy, but perhaps a more complete answer to satisfactory chimney cleaning problems than many lesser expedients.

Eternit Flue-pipes

There are still in current production flue-pipes whose performance, related to the potential outputs of many modern stoves, must be regarded as marginal. Those made by Eternit UK Ltd are seamless, have a clean, smooth, internal bore and can be cut with a fine tooth-saw.

These pipes will withstand a maximum temperature of 260°C (500°F) and are thereby vulnerable to damage by chimney fire.

Locking is by spigot and socket. Bends and terminals (cowls) are available and to provide additional insulation for external installation, flue-pipe covers are supplied with top and bottom closure pieces. These need no maintenance, are non-combustible, rotproof and durable. They are made of Nurastone – a cement-based material reinforced with alkali-resistant glass fibre which does not contain asbestos fibres. Nurastone has been submitted to Warrington Research Centre for a non-combustibility test in accordance with BS 476: Part 4: 1970. Eternit Flue Pipes in Nurastone generally comply with the requirements of BS 567 for Light Quality and BS 835 for Heavy Quality materials.

Even so, Eternit pipes made to this standard should only be considered as marginally suitable for Class 1 appliances.

The Isokern Reamer

A problem that often faces property owners is the irregularities that build up inside old chimney flues. These can be caused by brickwork moving with age, or by bricks falling away from the wall and lodging in corners. Often these obstructions are so acute that even relining with liquid concrete is not possible.

It may be that a chimney is too narrow to accept any type of liner, and the chimney may be structurally unsound and in need of strengthening. In more modern dwellings, the remains of old clay liners may obstruct the chimney.

The Danish Isokern company has developed a unique reaming tool which is now available in the UK on a rental basis from Kedddy Ltd. The reamer looks like a short-

Photo 100 A vertical view upward into two brick chimneys – that on the left has been reamed out by the Isokern reaming tool ready to receive 200mm liners

Photo 101 An Isokern reaming tool in action – seen vertically from above

ened naval torpedo with a propeller-like cutting tool at one end. A flexible drive operates this cutter, or reaming head, which is composed of chain grinders. Attached to the bottom of the chimney is a large industrial vacuum cleaner. The function of this machine is to drill out any existing chimney to a width that will allow matching chimney liners to be fitted (see p 122). By using chain grinders as a cutting agent, no vibrations or lateral forces are transmitted to the chimney walls during the working operation. The tool is automatically self-centring during the cutting programme and is capable of working around bends. All debris and dust is removed by the vacuum cleaner. It is usual for reaming and relining by this method to be completed in one day.

One particular advantage of renovating an old chimney with pre-cast chimney liners by this method is the structural rigidity that is restored to them. This reinforcement is stronger than that afforded by the refactory cement method.

Tests indicate that additional insulation is also afforded. During 1,000°C (1,830°F) chimney-fire tests a standard chimney's surface temperatures fell from 109°C (198°F) before relining to 43°C (109°F) afterwards.

Useful Addresses

Chimney systems and flues

Anki Chimney Systems
Kolind & Co,
Littleworth,
Norton Lindsey,
nr. Warwick CV35 8HD.

Brefco Superflue
PO Box 16,
Brookhouse,
Peel Green,
Eccles,
Manchester M30 7QA.

The Chimney Specialists Ltd
Jubilee House,
Mills Road,
Chilton Industrial Estate,
Sudbury,
Suffolk CO10 6XE.

Constructa Chimneys
Taylor & Portway Ltd,
52 Broton Drive Trading Estate,
Halstead,
Essex CO9 1HB.

Flue pipes

CICO Chimney Linings Ltd
Westleton,
Saxmundham,
Suffolk IP17 3BS.

Eternit UK Ltd
Meldreth,
nr. Royston,
Hertfordshire SG8 5RL.

Hepworth Stoneware Flue Liners
The Hepworth Iron Co Ltd,
Hazlehead,
Stocksbridge,
Sheffield S30 5HG.

Isokern Chimneys
Kedddy (UK) Ltd,
Red Lodge,
Bishopsgate Road,
Englefield Green,
Surrey TW20 0YJ.

Marflex Chimney Systems
(*see* Thermoflue Chimneys).

Parkabest, Parkachest, Parkaflue
and Rite-Vent Chimneys
Crowther Estate,
Washington,
Tyne and Wear NE38 0AB.

Selkirk Manufacturing Ltd
Selkirk Chimneys,
Bassett House,
High Street,
Banstead,
Surrey SM7 2LZ.

Thermoflue Systems Ltd
Unit 40,
Llandon Industrial Estate,
Cowbridge,
South Glamorgan,
CF7 7PB.

Cookers and boilers

Aga-Rayburn Stoves
PO Box 30,
Ketley,
Telford,
Shropshire TF1 4DD.

Baxi Heating
Bamber Bridge,
Preston,
Lancashire PR5 6SN.

Bosky Cookers
U.A. Engineering Ltd,
Canal Street,
Sheffield S4 7ZE

Country Cookers Ltd
5 Sherford Street,
Bromyard,
Herefordshire HR7 4DL.

Dé Longi Spa
31100 Treviso/Italia,
via Lodovico Seitz 47

Godin Cookers SA
02120 Guise,
France.

Oranier Cookers
Frank Aktiengesellschaft,
Postfach 1361,
D-6340 Dillenburg,
Germany.

Rosières Cookers
Usine de Rosières,
Lunery – 18400 St-Florent-sur-Cher,
France.

Stanley Cookers
Calfire (Chirk) Ltd,
Unit One, Acorn Industrial Estate,
Holyhead Road,
Chirk,
Clwyd LL14 5NA.

Tirolia Cookers
Tirolia-Blomberg,
S.F.A.S., The Airfield,
Winkleigh,
Devon EX19 8RH.

Trianco Redfyre Ltd
Thorncliff,
Chapeltown,
Sheffield S30 4PZ.

Cowls

Aspiromatic Cowls
The Chimney Specialists Ltd
(*see* Chimney systems).

Colt Cowls
Colt Building Products Ltd,
Progress Business Park,
Progress Way,
Croydon,
Surrey CR0 4XD.

Exhausto Fans
Strax Distribution Ltd,
41b Brecknock Road,
London N7 0BT.

O.H. Chimney Cowls
O.H. Ltd,
The Avon Centre,
Wallingford Road,
Kingsbridge,
Devon TQ7 1NB.

Smokex Chimney Fan
Kedddy (UK) Ltd
(*see* Chimneys systems).

Vedette Cowl
Prowoda Heat Ltd,
Southern Avenue Industrial Estate,
Leominster,
Herefordshire HR6 0QF.

Electric Firelighters

Grenadier Firelighters Ltd
Unit 3c,
Barronmore Enterprise Estate,
Village Road,
Great Barrow,
Chester CH3 7JS.

Thermoelectric Generator
TEG Products Ltd,
01 Todd Campus,
West of Scotland Science Park,
Glasgow G20 0XA.

Fireplaces and grates

Robert Aagaard Ltd
Frogmire House,
Stockwell Road,
Knaresborough,
North Yorkshire HG5 0JP.

A Bell & Co Ltd
Kingsthorpe,
Northampton NN2 6LT.

Brock's Fireplaces Ltd
Centurion Works,
Union Road,
Kingsbridge,
Devon TQ7 1EF.

Butterfly Brick Ltd
Wellingston Street,
Ripley,
Derby DE5 3DZ.

Galleon-Claygate Fireplaces
216/230 Red Lion Road,
Tolworth,
Surbiton,
Surrey KT6 7RB.

Hallidays Fireplaces
The Old Cottage,
Dorchester-on-Thames,
Oxfordshire OX9 8HL.

Marble Hill Fireplaces Ltd
72 Richmond Road,
Twickenham,
Middlesex TW1 3BE.

Flexible chimney liners

Chimflex
Rite-Vent Ltd,
Crowther Estate,
Washington,
Tyne and Wear NE38 0AB.

Multiflex
Marflex International Ltd,
Unit 40,
Llandon Industrial Estate,
Cowbridge,
South Glamorgan CF7 7PB.

Flue cleaners

Hotspot Chimney and Flue Cleaner
Hydrachem Ltd,
Unit 11,
Gillman's Industrial Estate,
Billingshurst,
Sussex R14 9EZ.

Fuel manufacturers

Extracite
Sophia Jacoba Handelsgesellschaft mbh,
PO Box 1320,
D-1542,
Huckelhoven 1,
Germany.

Maxibrite Fuel
Maxiheat Ltd,
nr. Mwyndy Works,
Llantrisant,
Mid Glamorgan CF7 8PN.

Gas heaters

Baxi Heating
(*see* Cookers and boilers)

Calor Gas Ltd
Appleton Park,
Slough SL3 9JG.

Dé Longi Spa, Italia
(*see* Cookers and boilers).

Trianco Redfyre Ltd
(*see* Cookers and boilers).

Valor Heating
Erdington,
Birmingham B24 9QP

Heating consultants

Sutherland Associates
Century House,
100 High Street,
Banstead,
Surrey SM7 2NN.

Insulation

Freeman Insulation
Willowcroft Works,
Molesey Avenue,
East Molesey,
Surrey SL3 9JG.

Multifuel stoves

Aarrow Fires Ltd
North Mill Industrial Estate,
Bridport,
Dorset DT6 3AH.

Bodart & Gonay
Rue de la Hoegne,
19 (BP-31),
B-4870,
Theux,
Belgium.

181

Charnwood Stoves
A.J. Wells & Sons,
Westminster Lane,
Newport,
Isle of Wight,
PO30 5DP.

Dé Longi Spa, Italia
(*see* Cookers and boilers).

Dovre Castings Ltd
Unit 81,
Castle Vale Industrial Estate,
Minworth,
Sutton Coldfield,
West Midlands B76 8AL.

Efel SA
Fonderies du Lion,
6373 Couvin,
Belgium.

Flameware Fires
Branbridges Road,
East Peckham,
Kent TN12 5HH.

Franco-Belge Stoves
(as for Dovre Castings).

Glow Worm Heaters
Hepworth Heating Ltd,
Nottingham Road,
Belper,
Derby DE5 1JT.

Godin Stoves SA
02120 Guisse,
France.

Hunter Stoves
Ravenheat,
Station Road,
Morley,
Leeds LS27 8JR.

Morsø Stoves
N.A. Christiensen & Co,
DK-7900 Nykøbing Mors,
Denmark.

Oranier Stoves
(*see* Cookers and boilers).

Stack Vista Stoves
Stack Manufacturing Co Ltd,
PO Box 9354,
Newmarket,
New Zealand.

Stanley Stoves
(*see* Cookers and boilers).

Trianco Redfyre Ltd
(*see* Cookers and boilers).

Vermont Castings Inc
Uunit 9,
Prime Industrial Park,
Shaftesbury Street,
Derby DE3 8YB.

Open fires

Baxi Heating
(*see* Cookers and boilers).

British Coal
Central Marketing Services,
Eastwood Hall,
Eastwood,
Nottingham NG16 3EB.

Dunsley Heat Ltd
Fearnought,
Huddersfield Road,
Holm Firth,
West Yorkshire HD7 2TU.

Esse Firemaster
Ouzledale Foundry Co Ltd,
PO Box 4,
Long Ing,
Barnoldswick,
Colne,
Lancashire BB8 6BN.

Flamewave Fires
(*see* Multi-fuel stoves).

Jetmaster Fires Ltd
Winnall Manor Road,
Winnall,
Hampshire SO23 8LJ.

Rene Brisach Cheminées
Route du Plan,
83120 Ste-Maxime,
France.

Paraffin heaters

Dé Longi Spa, Italia
(*see* Cookers and boilers).

Godin Stoves
(*see* Multi-fuel stoves).

Professional organisations

British Flue and Chimney Association
Sterling House,
6 Furlong Road,
Bourne End,
Buckinghamshire SL8 5DG.

National Association of
Chimney Lining Engineers
PO Box 35,
Stoke-on-Trent ST4 7NU.

National Association of Chimney Sweeps
PO Box 35,
Stoke-on-Trent,
ST4 7NU.

National Fireplace Association
Bridge House,
Smallbrook,
Queensway,
Birmingham B5 4JP.

Radiators

Clyde Combustions Ltd
Cox Lane,
Chessington,
Surrey KT9 1SL.

Finrad Ltd
62 Norwood High Street,
London SE27 9NW.

Myson Heating Radiators
Eastern Avenue,
Team Valley Trading Estate,
Gateshead,
Tyne and Wear,
NE11 0PG.

Sensotherm Europanel Ltd
Stafford Park 16,
Telford,
Shropshire TF3 3BB.

Zehander Steel Radiators
Invincible Road,
Farnborough,
Hampshire GU14 7QU.

Ventilators

Draughtmaster
Marshall & Parsons Ltd,
111 London Road,
Leigh-on-Sea,
Essex SS9 3JL.

Wood Stoves

Harrie Leenders haardkachels
Industrieweg 9a,
5688 D P Oirschot,
Holland.

Acknowledgements

If I were to list individually everyone who has helped me with this book, I should need another volume.

When I thank Laurie Pentzer of the SFAS, and David Malkin of WARM, I am thanking all their patient associates as well.

Jonathan Brind, editor of *Solid Fuel* magazine, has generously allowed me to ransack his files.

Among the press of private companies with whom I have had contact, three individuals stand out as having bent backwards to be helpful: Robert Colquhoun of Castle Heating, Odiham, Hampshire, has extended his aid far beyond the call of friendship; Peter Kelly of Kedddy, Egham, Surrey, secured for me from his company's vaults original artwork of great value; and Christian Pederson of Thermoflue, Cowbridge, South Glamorgan, has crawled up and down roof-tops at great risk to life and limb taking photographs that I needed.

To these, and all others, not here listed – I give my appreciative thanks.

Index